for Mum
Hope you
enjoy & thank
you for some of
the recipes.
love Lynne x

2015.

Lynne Allbutt © 2015

This edition of Allbutt's Allsortium, based on the original Allbutt's Almanacs (2012/2013/2014), published November 2015.

Follow Lynne on Twitter @lynneallbutt

www.lynneallbutt.com

Allbutt's Allsortium

A Nature Lover's Companion
and Gardening Guide.

Dedication:

With gratitude to nature for providing my vocation, recreation and retreat.

Nothing, no matter how good or how bad,

can fail to be improved by being out in the fresh air;

tell your troubles to the trees,

lay your fears down amongst the flowers

and share your secrets with the stars.

Recognise, respect and reconnect.

Give gratitude. Ask for guidance;

you may not receive anything straightaway

but then again you might ...

About The Author ...

Will grow in most conditions.

Enjoys full sun.

Requires a lot of space.

Dislikes being cut back.

Will not tolerate dead wood.

Provides year-round interest.

"Keep your appointments with nature;
how else will you meet with magic?"

www.lynneallbutt.com

Welcome to

Allbutt's Allsortium

As well as a 'guide for' I'd like to think of it as a 'celebration of' all the wonderful things that gardening and being involved in nature brings.

I personally owe a debt of gratitude to the great outdoors; it has enhanced, and often enabled, the good times and made the not so good times bearable somehow.

Not only has nature has provided me with my profession or vocation but also my recreation or 'play time'; and I don't mind admitting that I find it quite difficult to put my depth of gratitude and passion for the Natural World into words.

It is my heartfelt desire to keep promoting the benefits of nature, physically, mentally and emotionally and to re-introduce and remind people of the simplest ways to reconnect.

Sitting on the grass, walking in the woods, splashing about in streams and being able to identify and recognise the plants you mingle with; if we know the name of something there is a connection and we are far more likely to respect it.

It is great that awareness of global environment issues is being raised, however, let's not forget the plants and wildlife in our own back yards. This connection not only benefits that which is being observed but also those who are doing the observing.

Connecting with nature is like plugging into the most natural and organic energy there is and instigates a reconnection with intuition (tuition from within) and a universal energy which can only benefit us all.

I hope that 'Allbutt's Allsortium' will take us all a few steps closer to that connection.

Lynne Allbutt

A Few Ingenious Ideas
(traditionally known as 'Top Tips')

To have continuous colour in your garden, visit the garden centre at least once a month and buy something in flower or with colourful foliage.

Grow sweet peas amongst runner beans – both love well manured soil and the same sort of support system. Pick beans for the pot and flowers for the table.

Keep slugs out of container grown veg and Hostas by smearing Vaseline around the outside of the pot. Deep Heat also deters them.

Plant low growing herbs like thyme and chamomile in your lawn, especially under washing lines and seats as it smells lovely when you walk on it and when you mow the grass.

When planting bulbs, scatter them on the soil or grass first and plant them where they land – this will avoid planting them in straight lines and make them look natural when they bloom.

Old woolly jumpers make great organic (and colourful) liners for hanging baskets. Remember to ask first!

Put sheep's poo into a hessian sack and suspend in a water butt for an effective liquid fertiliser.

Use a snow shovel to 'rake' and pick up windfall apples. It's stronger than a rake and the apples don't get stuck on the tines.

Have fun! Sink a small flower pot into your lawn for golf putting practise. Use a spray line marker for instant games like hopscotch and running lanes on the lawn. It can be cut out next time you mow.

Don't stand under a hanging basket when watering it.

When designing and planning a path to the front door, remember that dogs and postmen take the shortest route.

Keep dead heading summer and winter bedding displays to keep new flowers coming – picking flowers for the house will also encourage new growth on many perennials and roses.

Feed birds in an open area to avoid 'cat'-astropic effects! Birds also need a supply of clean water in summer and winter; a birdbath is great entertainment for both bathers and spectators.

A man is more likely to want to do an outdoor task if it involves using something with an engine.

Putting a Viagra tablet in with the water of a vase of cut flowers will make the blooms last longer ... honestly.

Make the most of sunny windowsills and space in a

conservatory to grow your own veg and herbs.

Don't use a greenhouse as a shed ... get rid of it and get a shed.

When pruning lots of shrubs or roses, spread an old sheet or curtain on the ground; put all cuttings onto it to take away.

Mark the inside edge of an old pair of wellies with inch/cm marks to provide an instant ruler when planting or sowing seeds in the veg patch.

Unusual containers can make great displays when planted; try old wellies, boots, kettles, wooden boxes; be creative and don't forget to make sure there's a drainage hole in the bottom.

When draining a pond, always drain through a sieve to catch little snails and seeds.

Barefoot Forward

It is always a little difficult to identify the exact moment when my barefoot journey began. Of course some would say it was the moment I was born. For ease of explanation I tend to say it was at the age of 44 when I trained to run a barefoot 6K for charity. But when I poke my drifting memory, there were several chapters throughout my life where being barefoot had some considerable significance. Coincidence or missed sign posts? I can't say for sure but I believe the latter.

Either way it was in 2010 when I began to take relinquishing my footwear seriously. Challenges have been my preferred method of motivation in the past and this was no exception; I began training for a barefoot 6K run in Battersea Park. I am passionate about raising self awareness and have always had an innate drive to be at least within arm's reach of my potential as a

human being. On all levels. I believe we have to be able to nourish and nurture ourselves before we are able to care for anything or anyone else.

Self awareness and personal accountability have been my fuel. My respect and reverence of nature has been my fire, the passion I have been tending and feeding throughout my life and which has served me well as a result. I established a garden landscape and maintenance business at 17 years old and still run it today. Nature has provided me with both my profession and my recreation.

With hindsight, I think the 6k barefoot challenge was a necessary way for me to discover my barefoot path. I have always been very grounded and despite my adoration of the great outdoors, without the motivation of a barefoot challenge, I would have kept my boots on to enjoy the things I do, from dry stone walling to bee keeping.
And of course, heeding the gift of being ushered along my barefoot path, freeing my feet brought the most unexpected experiences and benefits. The answers which I were seeking were delivered in a way that the universe knew I would embrace the most effectively. And these answers are part of being able to 'play it forward', to be able to share experiences and findings with others, to encourage them to explore further and promote their own growth and healing.

There is a lovely saying, 'when we wear shoes our feet are blind and deaf'; we are indeed dismissing a valuable sensory organ. I didn't realise this as I began the intrepid steps of exposing my feet as much as possible to 'toughen them up'. I arrogantly thought I was re-educating them. Oh the irony. My feet became invaluable teachers as I ventured along my barefoot path. I decided I didn't want to continue to eat meat – my exact realisation was not to want to put 'flesh' into my system. Then my body told me it didn't want dairy products either, thank you very much.

These changes were made on a cellular level, by my body not my head. I think decisions made with the head lack authenticity and therefore are not easily sustained. Through my feet, my body had a new voice and I listened. It was a very organic, authentic and congruent procedure. It was on a cellular level; a return to a primal inner wisdom, tapped into through the nakedness of my feet. And not at all what I expected. Nonetheless I embraced the wisdom.

I didn't even query these requirements from my inner self; they were effortlessly integrated and sustained because they were as I was supposed to be. I was realigning with my true self. My clarity improved, decisions were arrived at easily and more importantly implemented with courage and grace. Improved clarity resulted in improved relationships and steadily my self worth and confidence grew too. I may have been the one taking action but there was no doubting the 'divine guidance'.

Whilst I retained my steel toes capped boots for work, I embraced the opportunity to take my bare feet and learning into other aspects of my life, including the media. My ego retreated. Ditching the safety and security of shoes makes one quite vulnerable, emotionally as well as practically. I felt exposed on an emotional level which was far more challenging than dealing with the practical issues. And yet that too was authentic and congruent. And necessary.

It seems that truth and vulnerability are congruent aspects of who or what we are; we need to expose our fears in order to heal. And once we start healing ourselves then we can begin to encourage and assist others to do the same. The other wonderful thing was that I was simply facilitating the healing, just allowing it – the earth, nature and divine wisdom was doing the rest.

Walking with bare feet is very meditative. You have to remain in the 'now', it is not a choice arrived at by reading nor imposed by a teacher. You have to look where you are going! That keeps you in the present; keeps you mindful. Organically. I believe it is 'being in the present' that provides, or just allows, clarity. We know what we 'should' be doing but incessant noise and distractions prevent us from hearing that quiet inner voice of intuition – tuition from within.

The clues are in the phrases we use – 'my heads all over the place', 'my heads in the clouds' or 'feeling my feet', 'standing my ground'. Information that is received via the feet is grounding, it can be trusted, it is from Source. And as it travels up through our body it is experienced by the heart before the head gets an opportunity to sabotage or distort it!

I have also always worked with elementals and nature spirits and regularly commune with plants, animals and even rocks; I found I heard their wisdom louder, clearer and stronger as a result of spending time bare foot. I treat and assist animals using Zoopharmacognosy (how animals self medicate in the wild) and again, had quicker and more effective results when bare foot. It is as through the earth provides a conduit for divine assistance.

Most of us are like a light that flickers on and off as the plug isn't in the socket properly and the connection comes and goes; connecting with the earth through bare feet is like pushing the plug in properly and making a good solid and consistent connection.

Whereas most people associate kicking off their shoes to relax, I now have to put mine on. Putting my feet back into shoes drops the connection which can sometimes be necessary. Sometimes I can receive too much energy, too much information. We also have to allow time to process this new information. I do this whilst shod.

Empowered by my new eating habits, improved clarity and increase in energy, I completed the 6K successfully and eighteen months later went on to set myself the bigger challenge of being the first person to run the width of Wales (52 miles) barefoot in 2014.

Then I wrote a book about it.

Having the courage, discipline and curiosity to spend time without the comfort, protection and security of my shoes and socks has become a pathway of learning, a journey of discovery and enlightenment. And one that fits nicely into my day-to-day life. We are gifted our appropriate pathways; the pathways we need to take in order make the discoveries we are here to make.

I can only encourage you to try it for yourself. I am not barefoot all the time. It isn't practical nor do I believe it is necessary. Spending any amount of time barefoot will evoke changes. Just sitting with your bare feet on the earth will also help. In its simplest form, this is referred to as Earthing or Grounding and there is much written about it.

Try to spend a little time each day walking barefoot outdoors. Incorporate it into your day. I always walk from my cottage to feed my chickens barefoot every morning. It is about 50 yards over flagstones, grass and a cinder path. Some days it is easier and more enjoyable than others but no matter what the weather or my level of enthusiasm I honour my morning barefoot walk; at least then, I have made my daily connection and feel more energised, and therefore equipped, to proceed with my day.

Despite my enthusiasm for sharing my experiences, some things have to be felt rather than explained.

Often when people now ask, "how does it work?" I just smile and reply, "Very well thank you.

Lynne's autobiography 'Barefoot and Before' is available from Amazon.

Horti-scopes
Horoscopes with horticultural flavour *(and birthday flowers)*

During years of gardening and being amongst nature I have
noticed similar personality traits appertaining to specific
'star signs' and have therefore devised *Horti-scopes* as an
alternative to the more familiar horoscopes:

Aquarius   20 Jan – 18 Feb   *Gladioli, bird of paradise, orchid*
Practical and hardworking, Aquarians don't like to spend
money on the garden and prefer to do the work themselves.
They love mowing the lawn as it gives them time to think
and will spend a lot of time in the shed. A good lawn mower
and time to use it is important for Aquarians.

Pisces   19 Feb – 20 March   *Violet, Poppy, lilac*
Pisceans have a short attention span and will have several
gardening projects on the go at the same time. They are
real nature lovers and wildlife and water are important in the
garden. Pisceans are good listeners and their advice is often
sought. Swings and hammocks will be appreciated in the
Piscean garden.

Aries   21 March – 19 April   *Honeysuckle, lilies, geranium*
As they are keen travellers, Aries gardeners need to make
sure they have good friends to water and look after the
garden whilst they are away on one of their many trips. They
love visiting big houses and grand gardens. Arians also love
fires, so will enjoy a brazier, or fire pit in the garden.

Taurus   20 April – 20 May   *Freesia, Rose, palms*
Appearances are important to Taurus people and they

will invest happily in their garden to keep it looking good. The earthy sign is very practical and methodical and will keep their garden neat and tidy. Often suffering with neck problems, they enjoy containerised gardening and prefer raised beds, pots and window boxes.

Gemini   21 May – 21 June   *Chrysanthemum, lilac, azalea*
Gemini people are animal mad, so be prepared to share the garden with animals of all shapes and sizes.   They are also sympathetic and terrific listeners, and the garden is used to regular visitors. Gemini's will always give you flowers or vegetables from the garden and love receiving new or unusual plants as gifts.

Cancer   22 June – 22 July   *White flowers, cow parsley*
Home life and children are very important to Cancerians. Their garden is a happy and busy place, with goal posts, balls and toys all over the place. They love food and will enjoy growing their own fruit and vegetables. As Cancerians have a tendency to put on weight, gardening will help them keep fit.

Leo   23 July – 22 Aug   *Sunflower, marigold, buttercup*
Leos love the traditional and conventional garden and are the most like likely to have their garden open to the public. Routine and familiarity is important. Leos have often inherited their house and garden and love having breakfast on the patio.

Virgo   23 Aug – 22 September   *Narcissus, violets*
Virgo people love keeping busy and their garden can often be neglected as they pursue other interests. They love homemade wines and cider and organic produce though

may not have the time to produce it themselves. They will often explain their haphazard garden as a 'wildlife garden'.

Libra   23 Sept – 22 Oct   *Large roses, hydrangea, mint*
Disliking change, Librans can appear to be lethargic and spend more time relaxing in the garden than working in it. They like the chic, courtyard garden style and can be quite artistic in a small space. They enjoy garden shows, keep good records and like labelling their plants.

Scorpio   23 Oct – 21 Nov   *Heather, honeysuckle, holly*
Scorpio gardeners love a bargain and will stock up on compost and seeds when they're on special offer. With high standards and a strong will, they like working alone and don't like criticism. They often worry about other people's reactions to new projects in the garden and will react well to encouragement.

Sagittarius   22 Nov – 21 Dec   *Pink tulips, blackberry, oak,*
Image is very important to Sagittarians and they like their garden to be admired, inspiring and full of colour. They change their minds often which reflect in their garden. Charming but temperamental, they enjoy good food and wine and will love entertaining outdoors but only with the very best garden furniture and accessories.

Capricorn   22 Dec – 19 Jan   *Ivy, baby's breath, pansy*
Capricorns call a spade a spade and are the most green-fingered sign of the zodiac. They are very hardworking and frugal but often feel unfulfilled. Capricorns are serious gardeners and can be intolerant of people trying to help. They age well, though may suffer with their knees; knee pads are a good investment for them.

Great Ideas for Little Green Fingers

Toddlers love to copy adults and to be involved with what's going on so it's an ideal age to introduce them to the joys of gardening.

There is also a great selection of gardening tools available from most garden centres for toddlers and young children to encourage them to get involved in the garden and learn at the same time. Simply having their own little watering can or brush will keep them engaged and involved whilst working alongside you in the garden. And for those with great aspirations, there are also mini wheelbarrows and toy lawnmowers to choose from.

You are never too young to 'grow your own' and bigger seeds will obviously be easier for little fingers to handle. Nasturtium seeds and sunflower seeds are large and are also quick and easy to grow providing the sort of swift results youngsters appreciate. Both the flowers and the leaves of nasturtiums are edible too – an added tasty bonus. There has been a bit of a revival of edible flowers and foraging of late and whilst some edible flowers may surprise you – dandelion, rose petals, daisies, clover and pea and bean flowers for example, it's perhaps a little unfair to expect a toddler to be so discerning and horticulturally aware so best not to let them graze unaccompanied!

In the veg garden, pumpkins and courgettes grow with the sort of vigour that impresses the young (and old) and pumpkins can obviously be utilised as Jack O Lanterns for Halloween too. Whilst small seeds are generally too fiddly for little fingers, the seeds of 'Cut and Come Again' salad leaves will tolerate being shaken enthusiastically over compost in a tub or large pot. Lightly cover with more compost (little green thumbs love getting dirty) and you will soon reap the rewards.

Or maybe sow little seeds in the shape of their initial; kids love the personal touch and are often impressed by using strips of old cloth or even stones or cardboard placed onto grass to spell their name. The material will also 'yellow' the grass making their name or word visible when the material is removed which is great fun; the grass will quickly recover.

Another easy way to encourage younger children out in the garden is to put up a simple little tent; it can be used as all sorts of things as their imagination allows and means they can go out in the fresh air when it's wet too.

Older children will also appreciate a space of their own so allow them room for a den or private area where they can meet or just hang out. Screen off an area with trellis, planting or simple brush screening and let it be an adult free zone. Swings and hammocks are great for teenagers as they allow 'deep-thinking, sulky swinging'.

Outdoor gyms are always good fun and can be created simply by hanging a speed ball or punch bag from a pergola or archway; encourage teenagers to be innovative by using a garden bench for tricep dips and incorporate 'step ups' on garden steps and a skipping rope on the patio for great outdoor circuit training.

A small rebounder can be dug into the ground so the surface is level with a lawn or decked area (a large trampoline can also be utilised in this way and although don't underestimate the amount of digging and hard work it'll take).

There are some great pieces of bespoke outdoor exercise equipment available now too so it's easier to create your own outdoor fitness trails or stations but you don't need to use money to lose weight; flex your mind as well as your muscles to incorporate fun ideas for fitness outdoors.

Breaking the Ice

As a writer and speaker, I think a good quote is like a ten stone penguin - a great ice breaker! Here are a few of my favourites:

Life without love is like a tree without blossom and fruit.
Khalil Gibran

To halve your gardening chores, marry a good gardener.
Oscar Wilde

Of course you can borrow my mower, as long as it doesn't leave my garden.
Ernie Wise

People are like wheelbarrows, useful when pushed but easily upset.
Anon

Don't knock manual labour; digging holes is one of the few jobs where you start at the top.
George Arthur

I was flattered to have a rose named after me until I read the catalogue description, "Good in a bed but better against a wall".
Eleanor Roosevelt

Suburbia is where the developer bulldozes out the trees and then names the street after them.
Bill Vaughan

Knowing trees, I understand the meaning of patience. Knowing grass, I can appreciate persistence.
Hal Borland

The best way to get enjoyment out of the garden is to put on a wide-brimmed straw hat, hold a little trowel in one hand, a long cool drink in the other and tell the man where to dig.
Charles Barr

The physician can bury his mistakes but a landscape designer can only advise his client to plant vines.
Anon

The true meaning of life is to plant trees under whose shade you do not expect to sit.
Nelson Henderson

To live life happily in the country one must have the soul of a poet, the mind of a philosopher, the simple needs of a hermit – and a good 4x4.
Anon.

Gardening is the purest of human pleasures.
Francis Bacon

Adopt the pace of nature: her secret is patience.
Ralph Waldo Emerson

I love to think of nature as an unlimited broadcasting station, through which God speaks to us every hour, if we will only tune in.
George Washington Carver

Despite the gardener's best intentions, nature will improvise.
Michael P. Garofalo

Guarding your Garden

A recent survey by a well known gardening magazine recorded the top five garden pests. Whilst it featured the more familiar, like slugs, snails and vine weevils, I think they forgot the most irritating garden pest of all – the garden thief. I often contribute to various crime prevention campaigns run by the local police force and am a great believer in prevention being better than cure. A secure garden is also a safe garden.

'Defensive planting', or planting prickly shrubs along boundaries and in other vulnerable spots will deter a two legged pest.

Old fashioned shrub roses are one of the most effective barriers and will also provide outstanding summer and autumn colour and interest with big blousy blooms and hips and haws respectively. They do take up quite a lot of room though, so the more traditional and compact hybrid T's will also do a good job and need less space or you could train a climber against a fence or trellis to form a thorny deterrent.

For a more informal look and a great harvest, consider planting prickly gooseberry bushes and even raspberry canes.

As well as prickly plants there are several other aspects to consider to keep your garden safe and sound.

- Repair all broken or damaged fence panels and fix gaps in your boundaries. Holes in a fence or hedge are like 'Welcome' signs to a thief.

- Consider placing trelliswork carefully. In the wrong place it can act like a ladder, allowing easy access for an intruder. Trellis work fixed to the wall of a house, for example, can provide access straight to a bedroom window.
- Large established shrubs and climbers on, or close to, a house can act in a similar 'ladder-like' way.
- Instead of locating a shed out of sight in your garden, re-think your design and incorporate it as a feature or focal point. This way it can be positioned within sight of the house making it a safer place to keep your tools and belongings. Paint it the same colour as an adjoining fence and also colour co-ordinate benches and other woodwork for maximum visual impact.
- Choose a building that is part shed, part summer house or add a pergola to a simple shed to enhance its appeal.
- Place benches carefully, they can often act as 'steps' to gain access over a garden fence or wall.
- Don't store valuable tools and things in an old greenhouse, where they're on full view; give the greenhouse away and buy a shed if you need the storage.

And if you are a fully paid up member of the 'it won't happen to me' gang, spend ten minutes totting up the value of your garden goodies and what it would cost you to replace it all. You'll be surprised ... and probably motivated, to 'guard your garden.'

Celebrity Chit-Chat with Pam Ayres MBE

Writer, poet and entertainer Pam Ayres MBE, confessed to me that despite often being a little overwhelmed by her garden, she still loves it dearly.

"I am lucky I have a beautiful garden and after being on the BBC's One Show it's now a TV garden," she laughed.

"It's very much a wildlife garden and I always choose plants that have added value for wildlife. Ones that will either provide a nesting site for birds, or nectar and food for insects. I've been keeping bees since 1996. My father and Granny kept bees and when my Dad died, my brother took on his bees. He said that my garden would be good for the hives, with the lime trees and other plants, so in they came. I have learned how to keep them from my brother. I only have 2 hives, which is enough. They're a lot of work."

As well as bees, Pam has 10 laying hens, 22 guinea fowl – "they just wander around, more for visual effect than anything else" – 8 sheep, 17 cows and two dogs of her own, a Jack Russell and a rescued large Munster Lander.

"I also look after my son and daughter-in-laws two dogs so I've usually got 16 muddy paws in the house." she laughed. "I'd love to have an animal shelter but if I did my husband would leave me."

A real outdoor lover, Pam gets out in garden or the fields most days. "We grow all out own veg and cut flowers too. I have got a gardener who helps but I love being outside and mucking in."

And when she's not busy at home, the cheerful small holder is busy promoting her autobiography, 'The Necessary Aptitude,' in which she shares that she started writing at just 12 years old. As humble as ever, she concluded, "I had no idea that I could use my vocabulary and love of words to make people laugh.

It's been such fun and irresistibly lovely."

www.pamayres.com

Raisin' an Eyebrow

A raisin dropped in a glass of fresh champagne will bounce up and down continually from the bottom of the glass to the top.

This is because the carbonation in the drink gets pockets of air stuck in the wrinkles of the raisin, which is light enough to be raised by this air.

When it reaches the surface of the champagne, the bubbles pop, and the raisin sinks back to the bottom, starting the cycle over.

Lonely Hearts:

A recent study has shown that one of the biggest killers in the West is heart disease, or dis-ease.

It may not be a surprise to many of us but what did surprise me is the notion that heart disease often starts with heart ache.

Or, more specifically, heart ache that is not remedied or resolved. We will all know what heart ache feels like and if managed appropriately, it will contribute to our growth and development.

Whilst we are unlikely to avoid painful and heart aching experiences, we need to be able to resolve issues of the heart as soon as possible and to 'move on'.

Heart disease is also be strongly linked to loneliness and a feeling of not belonging or being excluded; literally a lonely heart. Apparently, you can add years to your life just by joining social groups and meeting with other people once a week to play bridge, knit, learn a new skill or just to have a chat.

At the Conference of Consciousness and Human Evolution that I attended recently, Gregg Braden shared his experiences of living and working with various tribes and elders. Many people within these tribes were living to incredible ages, some were well over 110 years old. The oldest woman he met was a staggering 130 years old and had a birth certificate to prove it.

Gregg suggested that one of the reasons for such long healthy lives is the fact they have organic community support by belonging to a tribe. Loneliness or feeling excluded is simply not an option!

To think feeling left out or lonely can kill is shocking but not surprising.

The Ancient Essenes taught that our human bodies are actually designed to be able to function for around 900 years but, wait for it ... they also claimed that the first 100 years are the hardest as that is when we encounter the greatest emotional pain and hardship by losing everything that is dear to us people, pets, life styles and material stuff, to name a few aspects of things we treasure.

My great aunt lived until 107 and was incredibly bright and independent. She was also extremely pragmatic, strong willed and had a social life that still puts mine in the shade. I remember her saying, "Worry is like sitting in a rocking chair – it will give you something to do but won't get you anywhere."

Live life
like someone
left the
gate open!

Singing Plants

A few years ago, I spent some time at Damanhur, a spiritual community in Northern Italy which was founded in 1975 under the inspiration of Falco (Hawk), Oberto Airaudi (1950-2013).

As well as experiencing the magic of The Temples of Humankind, a subterranean cathedral created entirely by hand and dedicated to the divine nature of humanity and described as the Eighth Wonder of the world, I was privileged to learn about other esoteric projects which the Damanhurians are working on.

The Music of the Plants has been researched since as early as 1976 and came about from the desire to re-establish a balanced relationship with the environment and nature. Damanhurian researchers have created equipment capable of capturing electromagnetic changes on the surface of leaves and roots and transforming them into sounds. The plants learn to control their electrical responses, as if they are aware of the music they are creating and the result is a beautiful melody or 'plant song'.

I am fortunate to own one of the 'plant-to music' machines from Damanhur and have already had some wonderful experiences demonstrating the concept in various schools and offices.

Whilst at Damanhur I also learned how to 'orient' or realigned trees to the energy grid; another fascinating project, the Damanhurians believe the trees got so disenchanted with us that they simply 'dropped' their connection with humans.

By performing a simple exercise, we can encourage trees to 'come back on-line' and interact with us once again, sharing their knowledge and wisdom.
www.damanhur.org

Franken-Fruits

Often described as franken-fruits, there are several dual-fruits available from growers catalogues and supermarkets. You may know about strasberries, a variety of wild strawberry which looks more like raspberry or the pineberry, another variety of strawberry whose white flesh tastes like pineapple but what about cucamelons?

These little watermelon lookalikes are small enough to fit into a teaspoon, yet they have a big flavour of pure cucumber with a fresh tinge of lime and are a central American delicacy that has been enjoyed in Mexico for centuries. The strasberry was "born" in South America in the 1900s but virtually disappeared for the last half century until some Dutch growers rediscovered it; they also 'saved' the pineberry which had nearly become extinct in 2003.

Butter Me Up

It is so easy to make your own butter, everyone should try it! You will need:

- Double cream (how much you need depends on size and quantity of jam jars)
- Jam jar with lid
- Strong arms

Fill a third of the jar with cream; don't be tempted to add more, you need the room for the cream to expand before turning to butter. Screw on a lid and shake with all your might. It should take about ten minutes to turn into a yellow lump together with some creamy liquid.

The liquid is buttermilk and can be saved for making soda bread or scones. Run your lump of butter under a cold tap to wash off the remaining buttermilk and enjoy!

You can add a little salt if preferred or experiment with flavours like chilli, basil, and even ginger.

Undercover!

Flower Power

I am always endeared by the Power of Flowers:

Some of my favourites include Calendula, which is widely considered to be a lucky herb. It is said that if you place a bag filled with golden Calendula flowers beneath your pillow when going to sleep, breathing the fragrance of these flowers will enable you to dream of winning numbers and winning names. NB: I do not guarantee this!!

Alkanet is considered to be a good attracter of luck in business matters and folklore claims that this member of the borage family can also be burned as an incense against negativity.

The petals of the *dog rose* are believed to draw good luck in matters of the heart.

Some people believe mixing *feverfew* leaves with hyssop and rosemary leaves which they carry in their pockets or even a car, to prevent accidents.

The heart-shaped leaves of the Melissa officinalis, or *lemon balm*, suggest it is good for the heart.

The flowery tops of *meadowsweet* contain salicylic acid and is therefore considered to be 'nature's aspirin'. The sweetly scented flower is also thought to bring love, joy and a happy marriage.

It is thought that *nettles* were given their sting to protect themselves as they are so nutritious and useful. If cattle are fed nettles, they are said to produce more milk, and if given to chickens, they'll produce more eggs.

The leaves of the *periwinkle* are widely reputed to enhance conjugal felicity, pleasure, and happiness and can be sewn into the mattress to keep husband and wife forever in love.

At evening *clover* leaflets fold downward, the side ones like two hands clasped in prayer; add flowers and leaves to the bath water to aid in financial dealings of all manners.

Rosemary is widely thought to be a powerful guardian and can be planted by the front door to ward off evil .

According to legend, any place where *thyme* grows well is a place blessed by the fairies. In folklore the herb is said to be used to attract money. Fold notes around springs of thyme to make a little packet and keep in your purse or wallet.

Valerian is sedative to humans, but excites both cats and mice. The flowers can be put in bags and used to encourage love, protection and sleep. They can be used to aromatize their baths.

The Ancient Greeks considered the *violet* a symbol of fertility and love; people would place a violet leaf in their shoe and wear it that way for seven days believing they will find a new lover.

How's Ya Bean?

The humble broad bean has a broad variety of uses ...

- The very first young broad beans can be cooked in their pods; top and tail like French beans and slice to serve.
- Top leaves can also be used like spinach.
- Older beans, can be used to make a delicious pate (remove tougher outer skins).

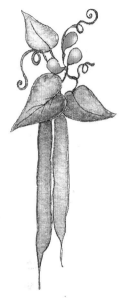

Broad Bean Pate

Ingredients:

- 350 g (12 oz) shelled broad beans approx.
- 175 g (6 oz) cream cheese
- Salt and freshly ground black pepper
- Sprigs of mint

Method:

Boil beans lightly in salted water until tender.

Mash or put through a vegetable mill with enough cream cheese to make a thick paste.

Season with salt and pepper.

Press into individual dishes and garnish each with a sprig of mint.

Serve with triangles of hot toast.

Or use as a filling in a chicken breast wrapped with pancetta.

Super Sunflowers

Sunflowers are one of the most uplifting sights in a garden and are great for all ages and abilities to grow. Plant next to a marked height chart or ruler to monitor how much they grow in a day!

The botanical name for sunflower is Helianthus; 'helios' meaning 'sun' and 'anthos' meaning 'flower'.

Sunflowers contain the chemical auxin which enables the flower-head to follow the path of the sun throughout the day.

The tallest recorded sunflower was grown in the Netherlands and reached 7 metres whilst the smallest was grown in Oregon using the Bonsai method and reached just 2 inches.

There is a huge range of varieties to choose from with colours ranging from pastels to a rich chocolate brown and if you want to try something different, check out Helianthus 'Teddy Bear' with its novel pom-pom blooms.

And don't forget to keep the seedheads for the birds.

Crackin' Nuts!

To avoid 'crushed nuts' put the nut *lengthways* and *horizontally* in the nut cracker so you are applying pressure from the tip and base (not sides) and you'll get a complete kernel every time!

Celebrity Chit-Chat with Alex Jones

One Show presenter Alex Jones is a familiar face on our TV screens and is also well known for sharing fashion trends on Twitter, but after a glamorous photo shoot we both did for the George Thomas Hospice's Celebrity Ladies Day Ascot Dinner a little while ago (see photo), she was as quick as I was to change back into jeans.

At the time she was working with kids on a Welsh series called Hip neu Skip (Hip or Skip) and admitted, "it's bliss going to work in jeans. It's great fun; it's a sort of Changing Rooms for kids.

"Apart from a tree house that we did, most of the makeovers have been indoors so far but we are planning to branch out to the garden. The kids love being outdoors. I'm sure being in the fresh air gives them even more energy.

"I love seeing what we can recycle in the gardens with the kids. They're great and always find a use for things the adults would throw in the skip. They don't know any different having been brought up not to throw things away.

"There are even places where you can take old furniture and they sell it for Charity, there's one near Pontypridd.

"The trend seems to be for 'shabby chic' now so that lends itself to recycling and using older pieces. We recently turned an old bath panel into a piece of art for the wall. You have to be creative – it's great to stretch the imagination. We also turned an old caravan into a den for a 15 year old so he could have his own space. I think that's probably the ultimate in recycling."

Alex also loves filming outdoors, "I love being out. I walk a lot. I remember walking up Snowdon with ex-boyfriend Matt and I had new boots on. It was so painful; I had to peel them off at the end. I still enjoyed it though. I love living in town but try to get out to the country to walk as often as I can. It's so good for you. I have worked a lot in North Wales and it's beautiful in the summer, I love the scenery there."

Alex still lived in Cardiff when we spoke and I wondered if her own garden was in line for a makeover?

"No, there wouldn't be room for all the kids," she laughed. "I call it a courtyard garden but Dad, Alun, calls it a path! I have room for a table and what I lovingly refer to as 'the forest', which consists of a pear tree, another tree but I don't know what it is, and a few tulips. The pear tree is lovely but when you're eating outside late in the summer the pears drop on your head. I've just put three stone-shaped solar lights in the garden too. They are pretty dim and don't give much light but they look pretty.

"Dad's good, he helps out a lot – when he was over last time he said something about a plant and mumbled, 'broom', so I went to get the brush, I thought that's what he was on about; I didn't realise there was a plant called broom! He also cleaned my car out for me when I first started travelling back and for to London," she added, "He's great."

Home is where the hearth is

Look deep into nature and you will understand everything better.

Herb Appeal

There are numerous ways herbs can help to improve your health, whether you simply sit amongst them to enjoy their fragrance and presence or whether you actively utilise them as medicine or food.

Try creating a herb chair or bench to sit on; use the crushed leaf of the Greater Plantain to relieve stings and bites and collect leaves, seeds, berries and even bark to make a delicious salad or tea tonic. Animals also self medicate with herbs and wild plants if allowed - dogs and cats chew couch grass for upset stomachs and cats adore rolling in catnip to stimulate or even sedate themselves as preferred. Even if you have no garden at all, your pet cat will appreciate sprigs of catnip placed in a tray in the house to roll in, crushing the leaves in the same way as they would in the wild. Dogs often choose to drink from muddy puddles as they need the algae they naturally contain.

Wild flowers and herbs not only benefit human beings but also our four-legged friends and birds too – chickens for example love chickweed which, not surprisingly, is also extremely good for them.

Indoors

We are probably all familiar with the benefits of having herbs and aromatic plants on the kitchen window for culinary use but don't forget the bathroom windowsill too; use a couple of leaves from potted plants like lemon balm, lavender, thyme and rosemary for example, to add to a running bath to release their own natural fragrant oils. Having plants on windowsills next to a sink also means they are more likely to get watered regularly!

Having a lavender plant in the house will help repel houseflies and the subtle relaxing fragrance of a lavender plant placed on a bedroom windowsill will also help you sleep.

Outdoors
There are also numerous ways in which to enjoy herbs outdoors as well as the more conventional herb bed. Although whilst we're on that subject, remember that when creating a herb bed outdoors make sure it's close to the house to make it more accessible and don't just restrict herbs to their own bed; the beautiful feathery foliage of fennel, for example, will provide interest at the back of a border and nasturtiums can be used to brighten up an old tree stump or transform a waste piece of ground. Whilst not classed as a herb, you can use both flowers and the leaves of nasturtiums in salads.

Planting chamomile and low growing thymes in the lawn, or even in between the cracks of paving on a path, will allow you to enjoy the aromatic fragrance which is released as you walk over the herbs or cut the grass.

Most herbs are also suitable for planting up in hanging baskets making them great to hang by the back door for cutting and harvesting as necessary. Choose evergreens like rosemary and thyme and even the less familiar Costmary, for interest through the winter.

Nutritious Nettles

Whether you respect them or resent them, stinging nettles are easily recognised by most people. The plant has a long history of use as a source of medicine, fibre and food:

Nettle syrup makes an excellent all round tonic or 'pick me up' if taken neat but can also be diluted with water to make a refreshing drink; use sparkling water and a slice of lemon for a 'posh' version.

Nettle Syrup
- 2.5 lb of young nettle tops (1kg)
- 2.5 pints water (2 litres)
- 3 oz sugar to 1/6th pint of water
  (80 g sugar per 100ml water)

Always use young nettle tops as if used when the nettles flower or start to go to seed they sometimes irritate the urinary tract.

- Put nettle tops and water in a large pan and bring to the boil.
- Simmer for an hour or so and strain to remove nettles.
- Transfer the liquid back to the pan and add appropriate amount of sugar (as above).
- Simmer for another 30 mins or until liquid thickens and goes syrupy.
- Cool and bottle.

The large amount of sugar will give the syrup a long shelf life.

Did you know the Latin name for the perennial nettle is Urtica dioica, from 'uro' meaning 'to burn'; the burn or sting can be relieved by rubbing in dock, mint or rosemary leaves.

Nettle Soup

1 tbsp olive oil
1 onion chopped
1 carrot diced
1 leek sliced
1 large potato diced
1 litre vegetable stock
400g nettle leaves
50g butter
50ml double cream

- Cook all the veg in the oil until softened.
- Add stock and cook for 10 minutes.
- Add nettle leaves, simmer for a minute or two until wilted.
- Blend the soup.
- Season to taste and stir in butter and cream to serve.

* For a vegan option simply leave out butter and cream.

Curry Flavour

This soup also doubles as a great curry sauce - fry off the curry spices and add soup!

Don't forget, 'Be Nice to Nettles Week' takes place in May.

Let's Dowse

Usually when I talk about dowsing, I get asked the same two questions: "What is dowsing?" and "How does it work?"

The British Society of Dowsers (www.britishdowsers.org) offer the following definition:

"To dowse is to search, with the aid of simple hand held tools or instruments, for that which is otherwise hidden from view or knowledge. It can be applied to searches for a great number of artefacts and entities."

Einstein himself respected dowsing and what it implied, although even he couldn't explain how it works.

He said, "I know very well that many scientists consider dowsing as a type of ancient superstition. According to my conviction this is, however, unjustified. The dowsing rod is a simple instrument which shows the reaction of the human nervous system to certain factors which are unknown to us at this time."

My own experience of dowsing and working with many experienced dowsers is that dowsers find what they are dowsing for and do so many times.

For me it is the results which matter not the reason.

Trust me, if you dowse successfully to find your car keys for example, you will be thinking more 'wow' than 'how?'

Sceptics, of course, say that dowsing doesn't work at all. Dowsers who seem to have a track record for success, they contend, are just lucky. But isn't luck something that happens when opportunity meets preparation?

Not everyone is a fan; Martin Luther said dowsing was "the work of The Devil" (and hence the term "water witching") however, some well-known names from history practiced dowsing, including Leonardo De Vinci and Robert Boyle (considered the father of modern chemistry).

I do believe that all things possess an energy force or field. The dowser, by concentrating on the hidden object, is somehow able to tune in to the energy force or "vibration" of the object which, in turn, forces the dowsing rod or stick to move.

The dowsing tool may act as a kind of amplifier or antenna for tuning into the energy.

You can also use other objects to dowse with, from a bespoke crystal pendulum to a washer on a piece of string, and I have also been able to dowse with just my hands which is a great experience.

If you are interested in learning how to dowse, there is endless information on the internet but tips that I found useful at the start include getting yourself into a receptive and positive state of mind.
Often if you are looking for something lost you will

be uptight which won't help! Similarly manage your enthusiasm, don't let ego override innate ability.

You do not make dowsing work; you must relax and allow dowsing to work through you.

Also ask the right question and focus.

And finally and most importantly, dowsers are doers, you will not learn to dowse just by talking or reading about it. You have to try, try and try again. Keep practising.

Practically, start by dowsing for something you know the location of, like water pipes leading to the house, so you get used to the feel of the rods or pendulum. Then ask someone to hide a coin under a rug, in long grass or just below the soil surface and dowse for that.

For the best result stay positive and have fun, the universe seems to like that!

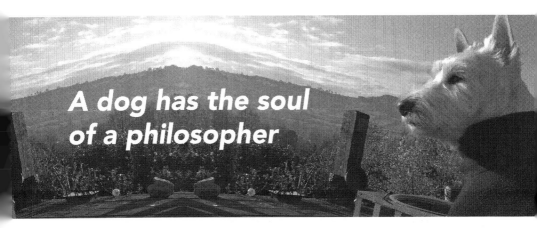

A dog has the soul
of a philosopher

Loving Labyrinths

The name Labyrinth comes from the Greek (maze of passages). However, although in modern English maze and labyrinth are interchangeable, in reality they are different.

A maze has many paths with lots of dead ends (multicursal), and a labyrinth has a single path which leads to a centre point, (unicursal).

Whereas their significance may be hard to fathom, research has shown that focused walking meditations are highly efficient at reducing anxiety and eliciting what is known as the 'relaxation response'. This effect has significant long-term health benefits, including lower blood pressure and breathing rates, reduced incidents of chronic pain, reduction of insomnia, improved fertility, and many other benefits. Regular meditative practice leads to greater powers of concentration and a sense of control and efficiency in one's life and labyrinth walking is among the simplest forms of focused walking meditation.

Labyrinths go back centuries and can be found all over the world; they are power centres, great for meditation and as an aid to problem solving and are also great fun and beautiful to look at.

They can be created out of all sorts of materials or simply mown into an existing grassed area; they are simply stunning when lit and used at night.

I have created many different shapes and sizes and all designs simply start by putting pen to paper. Remember the main objective is to create a continuous path to the centre and either use the same one to exit or create a new route. Have fun!

How to enjoy a Labyrinth:

1) Think of a question or 'challenge' you would like the answer to.
2) Enter the Labyrinth and walk the path to the centre as you focus on your question.
3) Pause in the centre for a moment or two and retrace your steps back out of the Labyrinth, being aware of any intuitive answers you may receive.
4) As you exit the Labyrinth you will (hopefully) have an intuitive answer(s) to your question.

NB: Although frequently asked, we have no proof that you will receive the Lottery numbers!

"Throughout the long history of Labyrinths, whenever and wherever society is going through rapid change and development the Labyrinth has blossomed. Now, humanity is seeking the sure path of the Labyrinth in an uncertain and confusing world."

Jeff Saward, Labyrinth Historian.

Sacred Circles

I have tremendous respect and reverence for stone circles and their magic.

It is thought that we may draw upon a consciously-created circle to realise goals and improve health and well being as containment magnifies our intentions. These circles may be known as medicine wheels, sacred circles, ceremonial circles or mandalas; the names are endless but the purpose is the same.

A sacred circle can be any size to suit your space and circumstance. Even a small circle created on a patio or balcony will help magnify intentions and energy. However, if you do have room in your yard or on the lawn to create one you can sit or stand in so much the better (though it will of course disrupt grass cutting.) It is important to remain focussed and positive during the construction. You are creating something magical and of beauty and it deserves reverence and respect every step of the way but of course, remain light and enjoy the process too.

If possible, create your circle within the waxing moon (new towards full) since this is a time of growing; constructing and building during a solstice or equinox will be even more powerful. Each circle will of course be unique and special.

You can incorporate four standing stones for each of the

directions, bury crystals at the centre or at the four points instead of standing stones, using citrine for East, rose quartz for South, smoky quartz for West, and clear quartz for North. Plants can be incorporated; depending on the size, an inner circle and 'spokes' can be added as can a 'central flame' or a 'meaningful' rock -at the centre of your circle. Please remember when you take a rock or stone from its present location, to ask permission of it. You will intuitively get a yes or no; yes is obviously OK, if you get a no, please leave it there. Making a little offering of tobacco is always a nice thing to do as you gather your rocks. You can also smudge your stones with a little sage or sweetgrass, individually or as a pile before you start creating the circle.

Dowse for the centre of the circle and to ensure the landscape is happy for you to proceed. Use string on a peg at the centre to keep the circle round and make sure it is an appropriate size. Begin building the circle in the East and work clockwise (sunwise). Remain mindful and positive. Use compass for directional accuracy and string for a round perimeter.

Give thanks for the circle and smudge it again if you wish.

Always enter and exit the circle from the East.

You can use your circle for meditation, manifestation, prayer and quiet contemplation. Just 'be and allow' and see what you feel and what you 'receive'.

Celebrity Chit-Chat **with Julian Clary**

Comedian and author, Julian Clary credits his father for his knowledge and love of gardening.

"My father tried to introduce me to manly pursuits like car mechanics and decorating but gardening was the only one that I was interested in as a child. And thank God I was. I know what a lot of plants are and all about deadheading and things.

"My triumph this year, were dahlias. I made a whole new flowerbed and planted about 100. They've been magnificent and I've been picking them from July to September. The house has been full of them, I'll grow more next year. I love the big red pom-pom ones, not the tight little mean ones. I grow spinach, garlic, lettuce, runner beans, tomatoes, it's all very rewarding and it's escapism for me.

"I don't normally talk about my garden, I like to keep it as a separate world. And I don't normally get asked," he added. "I like all the old fashioned cottage style plants like foxgloves, lupins and delphiniums but then I've also got lots of marigolds too.

"Jasper Conran is a good friend of mine and he is really upset by my marigolds, he says they belong on a roundabout in Reading but I'm keeping them anyway."

The enigmatic entertainer describes himself as 'very

outdoorsy'. "I became a rustic person 3 or 4 years ago when I got my chickens and ducks. They have the run of the garden in the day but are shut in at night because of the foxes. The fox killed 3 chickens last year and one still lives in fear. I had a guinea pig as a child but always wanted chickens, I love watching them in the garden; I find them delightful and pleasing. They only seem to dig in certain areas, they eat the bugs and fertilize the garden.

"I'm very into all of my flowers and there has been no conflict yet.

"I have also got two dogs, Valerie who is a 11 year old Whippet cross and Albert who is 18 months old and a Jack Russell and Staffy cross. They're so good for each other; Albert keeps Valerie active and she can be quite a calming influence on him in return.

"I am able to relax with my animals and my garden, it's such a contrast to my other life. I don't talk about it on tour or in my books, it would be incongruous. So there will be no jokes about Red Hot Pokers," he smiled.

www.julianclary.co.uk

Daffs to Dye For

For daffodils with a difference indoors, add a drop of food colouring to the water in the vase. As the daffs take up the water, the veins display the food colour with quite a dramatic effect. Red works the best, though blue is also quite effective.

Be warned though, food colouring will also colour everything else it comes into contact with – trust me!

Did you know that the daffodil is the symbol of good luck in China and of course is also the symbol for Marie Curie Cancer Care who host their Great Daffodil Appeal during March?

Flower Fizz
Elderflower Champagne

Ingredients:
- 20 elderflower heads,
- 1 kg sugar
- 2 lemons (juice and zest)
- 10 litres of water
- 2 tablespoons of vinegar

You will also need:
- Large bucket (to hold at least 12 litres)
- A sieve
- A funnel
- Muslin
- Plastic bottles (don't be tempted to use glass as a build up of gasses can cause them to explode)

Method:
- Boil 2 litres of water, pour into bucket and dissolve the sugar in it.
- Add the remaining 8 litres of cold water, lemon juice and zest.
- Add elderflower heads and vinegar and stir gently.
- Cover with tea towel and set aside for 24 hours stirring gently every 6 hours or so.
- After 24 hours, if it hasn't started to bubble, add yeast mix.
- Set aside for a further 5 days, stirring gently occasionally.
- Strain through a sieve and muslin and put into bottles.
- Leave for 8 days, checking the bottles occasionally and letting out excess gas gently if bottles are expanding.

Remember that folklore warns us of the Elder Mother's wrath and suggests that we always ask permission before picking any part of the elder tree.

Water Great Idea ...

Whilst elderflower champagne and cordial is extremely popular and can be found in many of the old hedgerow recipe books, I am a real 'sugar swerver' and prefer to take the healthier options when it comes to drinks. The flavours of the garden and hedgerows can still be enjoyed immensely in the guise of flavoured waters. It may not sound very exciting but I urge you to try it – they are simple and simply much better for you than sugary drinks.

And all you do is add water to fruit! Get a good sized jug, put your chosen fruit (mashing it up a bit normally helps releases the flavours) fill up with water and chill in the fridge. Fruits which work best include strawberries, raspberries, lemons, oranges, limes, watermelon and pineapple; adding herbs like mint and even basil add additional flavour; grated ginger adds a 'zing' and even cucumber will add a refreshing twist.

I use a lot of Melissa or bee balm too, just because it overflows in the beds and borders at my cottage. It is also great with hot water as a tea. I am also lucky to have copious amounts of wild strawberries – normally considered a bit of a pain as they are so invasive. I have let them go this year and am reaping the benefits of the heavenly scented little fruits. Not surprisingly, they are a great flavouring for water.

And try creating different 'blends' – strawberry and basil work well together as does orange, pineapple and ginger or just lemon, lime and mint. Slightly more exotic blends I have tried and which work include Jalapeno pepper and watermelon, apple and cinnamon and peach and mint. They are all made a bit more of a treat when made with sparkling water too.

According to the National Resources Defense Council, 90 percent of what you pay for a bottle of water goes toward packaging, shipping, and advertising and, as I have mentioned, flavoured waters just include added colours, sugars, and other unhealthy agents.

Water rip-off.

The speed of the leader determines the speed of the gang

Monthly Must-dos in the Garden

January:
Make the most of dry sunny days, to work off those extra Christmas pounds, by digging over the vegetable plot, or even creating a new one.   Leave clods of soil for the frost to break down naturally.

Continue to clear fallen leaves and other debris brought down by high winds and keep paths and steps clear for safety.

Go to the garden centre and buy a shrub or plant in flower to add colour to your garden. Don't forget that foliage and bark colour will provide interest too. Place any new additions in position in the garden but keep them in the pot. Keep relocating until you are happy they're in the right place, before planting.

Buying something that is in flower every month is a simple way of making sure you have colour or interest in your garden throughout the year.

Check out gardening magazines, books and websites for inspiration. Create your own Wish board/list.

February:
Check over all your gardening equipment and tools for the season ahead, repair or replace items as necessary.
Tidy up the shed, find the mower and prepare it for the

mowing period. You'll be glad you did once the grass starts growing.

It's a good month to plan improvements and reconsider various aspects of your plot. Compile a book of cuttings, pictures and notes of things you want to do in your garden this year. Make 3 lists – 'Must Do', 'Would Like' and 'If I win the Lottery' and fill the pages.

Pressure wash drives, patios and decked areas to get rid of moss and algae; don't forget your waterproofs.

Dead-head containerised winter bedding displays to encourage new blooms, and add a few new plants if necessary. It's worth it to raise your spirits at this time of year.

March:
Start mowing the grass, the 'first cut is always the steepest', as old winter grass is tough and wiry. Keep blades a little higher this month to avoid shocking the grass and the gardener.

Check pumps in ponds, (or put back if removed for winter) clean filters and start feeding the fish.

Prune roses (except climbers and weeping standards that only bloom once in the summer), invest in a good pruning book or ask an experienced gardener for advice, they always like to share knowledge. Sow parsley around the edge of the vegetable plot to keep slugs and snails off. Did you know, "Where parsley grows faster, the mistress is the master"?

Plant out early potatoes, use large tubs or special vegetable 'grow bags' if space is restricted. You'll be so glad that you did when you taste them later.

Jerusalem artichokes can be planted toward the end of the month. These architectural plants also make great living screens reaching 6-8 ft very quickly providing privacy and shade. The tubers make great soup.

Grow unusual vegetables, or even different varieties, like yellow tomatoes, blue carrots and striped beans to encourage children to take an interest. Give them their own plants or a little area to work. Treat them to their own gardening tools and clothing for Easter instead of chocolate.

April:
Sow seeds of hardy annuals in beds and borders directly where they're to grow. It's a quick and easy way of filling gaps and also a terrific way of temporarily camouflaging an area of waste ground or bare soil until you are ready to develop it. Nasturtiums make great ground cover, marigolds help stifle ground elder, Cosmos makes a great gap filler, and don't forget to encourage young green fingers to sow sunflowers.

Sort out watering facilities for later in the year, use water butts and invest in a system that allows you to connect a hose pipe to them. Also keep a watering can next to each water butt to avoid later frustrations.

Lightly prune shrubs that have finished flowering, don't be afraid of pruning; gather some advice and your courage and have a go!

Sow wrinkled-seeded varieties of peas, choosing a dwarf type if growing in pots or containers. Main crop carrots can also be sown this month. Remember that vegetables can be grown in beds and borders, carrot tops look decorative and runner beans can be grown up wigwams like sweet peas.

Consider introducing lawn edging to prevent soil from crumbling into beds and spilling onto paths and drives.

May:
Stake herbaceous plants in the borders, as necessary. It is far better to let the plants grow through the supports rather than try to revive flattened flowers later. Growing plants close together will avoid the need for staking and provide a riot of colour.

Sow runner beans in well prepared site and alternate with sweet pea plants for great colour later on.

Sow lettuce and salad leaves and remember these will even

do well in window boxes or tubs on the patio. If you are new to growing vegetables, start slowly and build up your confidence and although it sounds obvious, grow the things you like.

Summer bedding can be planted out at the very end of the month when all threats of frost have passed.

Try hanging baskets with a difference by planting with tumbling tomatoes, dwarf vegetables and/or herbs for great conversation pieces.

June:
Usually a very busy month in the garden as everything is in a rush to reach its potential! Don't worry if things are moving faster than you are, you'll catch up.

Keep the grass cut and keep tying in climbers and ramblers to keep the garden looking tidy.

If you can remove faded flower heads from beds and borders, you will encourage new growth and more flowers which will take the focus away from the things you haven't got around to.

Yellowing foliage can be removed from daffodils if it comes away easily. Don't 'rip' it off as the bulbs need the nutrients from the leaves for next year's displays.

Moles are often a problem this month as they search for worms, there are numerous 'suggested' methods of deterring them including putting ferret or badger droppings down the mole run. Both are the natural predators of the mole and their scent will send them scurrying to safety.

In sultry weather, add fresh water to pools and ponds with a hosepipe and spray attachment. This will oxygenate the water and lower the temperature which is particularly important in shallow pools.

July:
A good month to actually enjoy your garden, take time to just sit and relax a bit. Also cut some flowers for the house, a garden should be productive and having a vase full of your own grown flowers indoors will encourage you to grow more.

If you are barbequing, add a few sprigs of rosemary to the coals for added flavour and aroma and don't forget to use your mint in the Pimms!

Try to visit a few other gardens at this time of year, it's a great way to renew inspiration and get new ideas for your own plot. Add an outdoor mirror, paint the fence or shed to match the house, plant low growing herbs in the lawn (or around the washing line) so your footsteps or mower activate the beautiful scents, or simply hang a swing from an established tree.

Continue to deadhead spent blooms in the borders and containers and cut back herbaceous plants that have finished flowering completely. They will often reward you with a second flush of blooms. The exception are paeonies as they need to die back naturally.

August:

If small pots or hanging baskets have dried out, submerge the whole container in a large tub or dustbin full of water. Bubbles will be released as the compost reabsorbs the water; keep submerged until the bubbles stop.

Keep picking sweet peas, even if it means giving them away – people love receiving them - as once they form seed pods the flowering period will grind to a halt.

If you are going away on holiday, arrange for someone to take care of watering your containers and picking vegetables (and sweet peas). If you're lucky the latter will be payment enough for the former.

Invest in some outdoor entertainment; garden games are more readily available now, from large Chess sets to outdoor Twister. If you have the room, a zip slide is great fun although outdoor trampolines have proven to be a deterrent to next-door house purchasers.

To have new potatoes for Christmas Day lunch, plant late cropping (second crop) potatoes at the end of the month. Treat as normal but cover with fleece during frosty weather. If you only want them for Christmas, consider using a large container for ease.

September:

Plant spring flowering bulbs (tulips are best left until October) this month. If containerising, plant in layers for maximum flower displays. If naturalising daffodils in grass, remember you won't be able to cut the grass until the leaves have died back, which can look untidy. To avoid a regimental look, scatter the bulbs on the surface and plant where they land.

Dwarf varieties of bulbs are fantastic in window boxes and containers and even hanging baskets, especially if planted with decorative ivies.

Bulbs for forcing indoors can be prepared now to bloom over Christmas. They also make great presents for children to give to favourite Aunties.

It is important to give fish high protein food during September and October as they don't feed through the winter, relying totally on the reserves they build up now. Stop feeding fish in November when the temperature falls.

Give lawns a little tender loving care, reseeding or turfing worn patches and spiking waterlogged areas.

Using a purpose made lawn edging will stop soil edges crumbling into beds or onto drives.

October:
Put a net over pools and pond to keep out fallen leaves as these will rot and release toxic gases if left to build up. Try to keep on top of clearing leaves, especially on steps and paths and lawns. Don't wait until the last leaf falls, as

this makes clearing up a mammoth task.

Compost leaves where possible, remembering oak leaves take much longer to rot down than most others, so should be kept separate if possible.

If not already done, remove summer bedding and replant containers for winter and spring displays. Include small evergreen shrubs in larger containers and herbs such as rosemary and thyme can be utilised if close to the kitchen door.

Cut back spent growth of herbaceous plants in beds and borders. I like to leave flower heads on astilbes and sedums as they look great when frosted in the winter and old hydrangea flower heads should be left on for winter protection.

Remember that many insects use hollow stems and little leaf piles to cwtch into for the winter; a good reason (if you need one) to postpone the big clear up.

November:
Tie in climbers as necessary and check all structures in anticipation of stormy wintery weather.

Check stakes on newly planted trees and large shrubs and make sure all window boxes and hanging baskets (if used for winter bedding) are safe. Tidy away, plant supports and containers that are not being used.

Clean off all tools and the mower before you put them away.
Don't leave two-stroke petrol in a mower as it separates
during the winter and can cause problems next season.
Check electric cables before storing neatly with the circuit
breaker.

Check bonfires before lighting as they are an ideal habitat
for hibernating hedgehogs and please be considerate of
pets on Bonfire Night.

Overhaul pumps used for waterfalls and fountains and
remove submersible pumps from ponds. Clean them and
store in dry place for the winter.

Take care to prevent ponds and pools from freezing over
during the winter. It's important to let toxic gasses escape,
to avoid the fish from being suffocated and to avoid
pressure building up in a concrete lined pool.

Never smash the ice on a pond as the shock waves can kill
fish and the broken ice lowers the water temperature.
To stop a pond freezing over totally, keep a football or small
ball on the water surface or cover part of the pond with
boards or matting.

December:
Write out your own Christmas present list.
Distribute it widely.
Check out Garden Centres, shops, catalogues and internet
for Gardening Gifts for friends and family.

Packets of seeds are great little 'tokens' and are easily
enclosed with a Christmas card. *(See below).

There are numerous publications that can be subscribed to
as a gift, vouchers are always good for the unimaginative
and undecided, gardening gloves are always useful, as are
the many preparations to combat weather-beaten skin.

A garden Diary or 'log', is a good choice for the serious
gardener and garden games for the less serious; there are
funky wellies, floral gardening tools, solar powered radios,
pocket multi-tools and beautiful smocks, trugs and baskets
to keep it all in.

Presents that benefit our wildlife, as well as the recipient,
are a fabulous idea, choose from a nesting box with a
camera inside to monitor nesting birds and their young, or
a decorative birdbath, or even a selection of feeders to dot
around the garden.

And for the person who has everything, why not buy their
bird food for them ... it might not be the most conventional
present but useful and appreciated several times.

*Packets of seeds make lovely little presents to slip inside
any type of greeting cards and are nice to receive.
Choose from the exotic to the practical or try to match a

name or other connection – be creative and have fun, here a few examples to start you off ...

Heard you haven't BEAN well;   Forget-Me-Not;   Hap-PEA birthday;   Sorry I haven't BEAN in touch;   Good LEEK; You CARROT be serious !   You look RADISHing.

If you have saved seeds from your own plants, then send those as gifts for an even more personal touch. Photos of flowers and plants from your own garden can quite easily be turned into greeting cards too. Create your own range.

Happy Birthday - in dog years you'd be dead!

Flutter Bys

Prince Charles refers to butterflies as 'flying flowers' - they are certainly as uplifting as a beautiful bloom.

Whilst some of the smallest butterflies, like the 'Blues', only live for a few days, butterflies which can over-winter, like the 'Monarchs', can survive for nine months. But most butterflies only have a lifespan of two to four weeks, during which time it will focus all of its energy on just two things - eating and mating.

Did you know ...?

Butterflies nor bees can drink from deep or open water as the surface tension won't hold them, so they like to sip from shallow water, wet sand or mud. Providing a saucer (or even an upturned dustbin lid) filled with wet sand or mud, or simply placing flat stones in the water for them to rest on to drink, will keep them happy in your garden.

When butterflies bask in the sun with their wings open, they are increasing their body temperature in order to be able to fly and feed. They cannot fly if their body temperature falls below 86 degrees.

Some butterflies have a top speed of 12 miles an hour and most only live between 20 and 40 days.

Celebrity Chit-Chat with Radio 2's Lynn Bowles

BBC Radio 2 presenter, Lynn Bowles got half way through her practical year studying agriculture before she realised it wasn't for her. "It wasn't because of the bad weather or anything", she said adamantly, "Being Welsh I'm used to the rain; I'm Welsh and waterproof", she laughed. "I just thought it's not for me and I decided to do a degree in communications instead."

Well known for presenting her traffic reports on Radio 2, Lynn added, "We all spend too much time whinging about the weather. My philosophy is, 'if it's dry get outside and enjoy it – quickly.' Make the most of the good days." She explained, "I've only got a little terrace garden in London but it is all ready to be enjoyed and used whenever the weather's good.

"It was just a patch of grass for years, I'm not a great gardener but one day I just thought this is so rubbish, I have to do something about it. A good friend helped me and she did such a good job it totally changed my view about gardens and gardening. I hate the way those home programmes call a garden an outdoor room but it is - I call it the green room now!

"When the weather's good, we sit out under the olive tree", she said proudly, "and there's a great Prunus. I love it; it's got something going on all year. In winter it's architectural with great stems, in the spring there are delicate little flowers, in the summer the bark is a wonderful auburn-copper colour and the leaves are colourful in the autumn. I also like the New Zealand Flax, its good all year. I like value for money," she laughed. "I kept a bit of grass too," she admitted, "being Welsh I have to have a bit of the green stuff underfoot."

When I commented on her knowledge of plants she was honest, "I've learnt that you only have to know a couple names or facts in any subject to sound like an expert. I think I've told you all I know about gardening now."

The Cardiff born presenter has another confession, "Although Terry (Wogan) said I'm from Splott, it's not true. He just loves the word and of course it rhymes nicely with Totty, hence me being referred to as the Traffic Totty from Splotty," she laughed. "It's a great part of Cardiff though", she added quickly.

"Another of my favourite areas in Wales is the Gower. I only discovered it about 3 years ago and I love it. It must be one of Wales's best kept secrets", she enthused. "I went to White Sands and there was no one else there! And the countryside is so green, which is another reason that Welsh rain is good," she laughed. "Spain might be nice and hot but the grass there is yellow.

"I will move back to Wales one day; if my passport doesn't expire and I'd like to have a proper garden then. I'd like to do veggies and I think everyone should do their bit toward being self sufficient. I just hope it doesn't turn out that I've got black fingers.

"My Uncle Joe had the fastest donkey in Cardiff in the 1920's," she added proudly, "so I think I'll have to have donkeys too. It'll be a bit like The Good Life."

The Devil's in the detail

Moon Wisdom: Following the Rhythms of Nature

The cycles of the Moon have a powerful influence on the body, mind and emotions. The body is mostly made up of water and we are all influenced by the Moon just as the tides and plants are affected in nature. As the moon pushes and pulls the tides, we are also influenced through the effect on our body fluids and cells.

Depending on how hydrated you are and how balanced your electrolytes are, a full moon particularly can cause aggravation for people in the nervous system and cellular tissue. If the body is lacking in water and has a deficiency in potassium or magnesium, it will get stressed at times of particularly strong gravitational pull such as full moons and lunar eclipses. Staying well hydrated will help you remain more balanced through the moon cycle.

There are four different moon phases that cause distinct effects in our bodies throughout the month.

New Moon

New moon or dark moon (from the day of the new moon, to 3½ days later) is when the Moon is directly between the Earth and the Sun and therefore hidden. This is a time for rest, leading into new beginnings and new undertakings.

At new moon, the body's ability to detoxify is stronger than throughout the rest of the month; its absorption rate is lowest too, so it is advisable to have a break from any supplements during this moon. This allows the body to have more energy to clear out. The new moon is the most effective time to cleanse, fast, and also to start afresh, as new habits, new eating plans, or abandoning old habits will have a more powerful effect if put in place at the new moon. It's a time for giving thanks, reviewing old goals and getting ready to set new ones as you move into the waxing moon.

Waxing Moon

Waxing moon means the Moon is getting larger in the sky, moving from the new moon towards the full moon. The period of the waxing moon lasts about 14 days.

At this time the Moon represents the Goddess in her Maiden aspect. This is a time for growth, expansion, and working on positive change. During this phase the Moon is increasing and so is the absorption in our body; the cells can take in more nutrients due to fluid increase and electrolyte balance. Take in lots of healthy food to provide your body with nutrients, and supplements if applicable.

Limit your intake of toxic substances, as you will feel their effects more when you take in foods that don't work for your body type. Cut your hair during the waxing moon to promote growth. Crops that are grown for their leaves, flowers, or seeds should be planted or sown during this phase. Begin new projects that will bring new things into your life for both the long and the short term; conceptualise ideas and put them into motion, become engaged, make plans, work on increasing business, attracting customers or furthering your career. This is also a time for spontaneous and instinctive action, during which transitions may seem to be accepted more calmly than at other phases. Take this opportunity to make the changes you want to make.

Three phases of the waxing moon:
3½ to 7 days after the new moon: gather information and resources, make plans, lay foundations, start the change.
7 to 10½ days after the new moon: courage and motivation – add that little bit of extra steam. Decisions, balance. Trust your intuition.
10½ to 14 days after the new moon: patience (in preparation for the full moon). Plans seem to experience a pause; it's a phase of gestation. Movement and action may not be visible, but are occurring. Tie up any loose ends.

Full Moon
Full moon is when the Moon has reached its zenith, and forms a perfect sphere in the sky. The period of the full moon lasts from the day of the full moon till about 3 days after the actual full moon (sixteen to nineteen and a half days after the new moon). At this time the Moon represents the Goddess in her Mother aspect. We are at our fullest when the Moon is full – our weight increases as we hold more fluid and nutrients in our body. Absorption rates are at their highest (including of toxins, so avoid them if possible).

For women, the full moon is the ideal time to have a period, as the body has more nutritional balance and any nutrients lost through blood flow will not deplete the body too severely. This is the climax of the moon energies and major workings should occur. The full moon makes us highly sensitive: our senses are heightened, and so is the activity of the mind. It's a very intuitive and productive time, especially in terms of creativity, beauty, money, love, matters of the home, psychic abilities, dreams, and meditation. It's the ideal time for creativity and writing; but it can also generate random thoughts! Hence it's a good time for spiritual practice and focussed meditation too. It's also a time of heightened feelings, so bear this in mind when making major decisions as they may be strongly coloured by emotions.

Waning Moon

Waning moon means the Moon is decreasing in size, moving from the full moon towards the new moon. The period of the waning moon lasts about 14 days. At this time the Moon represents the Goddess in her Crone aspect. In this phase the body naturally cleanses and detoxifies, and clears the body of anything that's not needed in the system. We weigh less during this phase, because the body doesn't absorb or retain as much. It's a good time for cleansing regimes, diets and eating less, as our appetite is naturally smaller.

The process of letting go and emptying out is physical as well as emotional. In this phase, make a conscious effort to increasingly make time and space for rest, reflection, meditation and getting ready for the rebirth energies of the new moon. The waxing moon is focussed more on outer matters and instinctive growth, whereas the waning moon causes us to turn inwards and work through a conscious process of creative release. It's also the right time for hair cuts to slow growth and keep a hairdo, as well as dying one's hair. You should plant crops that are grown for their roots now.

Three phases of the waning moon:
3½ to 7 days after the full moon: review endeavours, give thanks, correct mistakes, settle disputes and make amends. Start taking things apart, and working on removing obstacles.

7 to 10½ days after the full moon: consciously let go of any negativity and anything that is causing obstruction; remove yourself from situations, relationships, and habits.

10½ days after full moon to new moon: increasingly rest, reflect, and prepare for the new moon energies.

New moon abundance ritual
The new moon phase – especially when combined with an eclipse - is the most perfect time to do an abundance ritual for the coming moon cycle.

Take a cheque from your cheque book, and write your name against the "Pay" line. If the idea appeals to you, write a little tagline by your name, something that describes you being your best self, eg: "Joe Bloggs, visionary business creator!"

- Either leave the date blank, or write today's date.

- Where you would write out the amount, write: "Paid in Full" and try and remember not to draw the squiggly line to block out the rest of the space. No limitations!
- In the box where you would write the amount in numbers, write "Paid in full", again without squiggly line.
- On the signature line, you can sign yourself, or sign "The Universe", or sign "The Law of Abundance" – whichever feels best to you.
- Now put it away in a safe place and forget about it.
- If you do not own a cheque book, just draw a cheque on a piece of paper.

By doing this mini ritual you focus your mind and emotions on what you want to create in your life.

The main thing is to set an intention with clarity, and create a vibration that you put out into the universe. You don't even need to believe that it's going to work – just do it.

You have nothing to lose even if you do not believe in magic!

Do it for a few new moons and see what happens.

Feast and Fast

Fasting is the voluntary absence (or reduction) of food.

I indulge in a 'wood fast' a few times a year, when I go, with my dog, camping in a remote woodland for three days and two nights with just water (and dog food for Yogi!).
No phone, no watch, no food and no people. It is a great way to realign and detox.

Calorie restriction, to just 500 per day, is one of the few things that has been shown to improve health and extend life expectancy.

One area of current research into diet is Alternate Day Fasting (ADF). It involves eating what you want one day, then a very restricted diet (500 calories) the next, and most surprisingly, it does not seem to matter that much what you eat on non-fast days.

The results of brain scanning in the US revealed something far more interesting. They discovered that hunger actually created new brain cells and so by fasting you actually increase your cognitive abilities. So fasting is exercise for the brain - hunger actually makes you sharper.

We take vacations, we have weekends off from work, we rest our tired bodies through sleep, and we "take a break" to rejuvenate from stress. One thing, though, that we hardly ever do, is take a break from food for any significant length of time.

Our digestive system requires high amounts of energy; therefore, it makes sense to give it a vacation once in a while.

Have you noticed that when you're sick, your appetite diminishes? Similarly, when animals are ill, they lie down and often don't eat or drink. Energy goes towards healing our bodies instead of digesting food.

Alternate Day Fasting is proven to be the easiest method to feast and fast – interestingly you want to eat less on the feast days.

On fast days have:
- Raw food diet of fruits, vegetables, seeds and nuts
- Vegetable broths
- Only fresh pressed vegetables/fruit juices
- Only salad (NO DRESSING!)
- An easy way to start – have an early dinner and refrain from food for a 16/18-hour period before eating breakfast – gradually work up to a 24 hr period ... for maximum effect work up to fasting for 2 consecutive days per week.

Or indulge in a wood fast!

Some people fight aging.

Not me.

I am happy to look this way.

I've travelled a long way and not all the paths were easy.

Seedbomb, Seedbomb;

You're my Seedbomb ...

A seed bomb is a little ball which consists of everything needed to grow a plant. The growing medium provides a good source of food and nutrients to give the seedlings a good start in life. When dropped or thrown on the ground in Spring-Summer-early autumn, they will be exposed to the right conditions to aid germination. They are perfect for planting on inaccessible places, wasteland and abandoned disused areas, or ugly roundabouts or simply drop them in your own garden. They can be laid out on bare ground or in pots or trays on a windowsill with water and enough light they will germinate and grow. Thin seedlings as necessary to allow for the stronger plants to flourish.

They are NOT EXPLOSIVE and NOT EDIBLE!

THE SEEDBOMB BASE RECIPE

Ingredients (makes 6 sizeable seedbombs)

- 5 Tablespoons of seed compost
- 4 Tablespoons of terracotta clay powder
- 1 Teaspoon of seeds
- 1 Teaspoon of chilli powder as a pest deterrent (optional)
- Sprinkles of water at intervals (i worked out it was about 20ml)
- Liquid fertilizer - if nitrogen, phosphorus and potassium (npk) are absent in the compost

This recipe is based on poppy seeds as a size guide.

If using larger seeds you should increase the volume of your ingredients to accommodate these larger seeds.

TIP: To make larger quantities of seedbomb mixture, use the same proportions but measure using larger containers, and use a bigger bowl!
You will need
- A bowl
- A strong spoon
- Kitchen towel or egg box
- Water
- A pen
- Your hands and some elbow grease
- An apron if you're worried about your clothes

Just Add Chilli
You can add natural non-toxic pest deterrents to your seedbomb mix, such as dried chilli or cayenne pepper, to keep those creepy crawly munching ants off your seeds!

And now for the mixing and making ...
1. Pour the compost into your bowl.
2. Pour the clay powder into your bowl.
3. Pour in the seeds.
4. Stir the dry ingredients together until well mixed.
5. Add water in small amounts at a time, mixing and adding until you form a dough-like consistency that sticks together nicely (not too sticky and not too dry).
6. Separate the mixture into six even lumps.
7. Roll each lump into a smooth ball.
8. Place the finished seedbombs on something absorbent like kitchen roll or an egg box.

TIP: When rolling your seedbombs, keep your palms flat to get a rounder shape. If your palms are slightly cupped, you get a shape not unlike a spinning top. Use your fingers to adjust the shape until you are happy with it.

What to do next ...
When you have made your seedbombs, you can:
1. Launch them immediately (if it is the right time of year); they will germinate quicker because they are still moist. Let them dry for a couple of hours so they are not too squidgy and don't lose their shape.
2. Dry them for up to 48 hours. The seeds will remain dormant until activated by water. They can be stored for up to two years and beyond, though some seeds may not germinate if left too long, especially vegetables.

TIP: Dry your seedbombs on a sunny garden wall, shelf, windowsill, radiator or in the airing cupboard.

Pour your ingredients into a bowl and mix well.
Add water slowly, mixing until you have a dough-like consistency. Separate the mixture into even lumps and roll between your palms to form a smooth ball.
And launch!

Huge thank you to the wonderful Josie Jeffery for her Seedbomb recipe.
www.seedfreedom.net

Celebrity Chit-Chat with The Barefoot Doctor

Stephen Russell is better known to most as The Barefoot Doctor, one of the leading figures in self development and who also has a healthy respect for nature.

When I met up with Barefoot (as he is fondly referred to) he explained, "We're all involved with nature, how can we not be? It is all around, we are Human Nature. If you live in the country you maybe more aware of nature on a day to day basis but even if you live in a city it is important to remember that you are still part of a big planet and universal energy, not just the man-made sculpture in which you live. We are all engaged in a huge adventure, part of a huge continuum. We are all atoms, all emotions, even the trees and the stars. We are all in touch with nature; plants animals, people are all one energy, one presence.

"When I spent time with the Native American Indians I had no practical knowledge of gardening or growing things but I got by as a healer by understanding which plants support us. Calendula (marigold) will heal all sorts of lesions, just drink it as a tea, it's magical. Lavender will help you sleep; dried chrysanthemum as a tea, is also a good tonic and will cool the liver, easing problems caused by eating rich foods."

Author of 14 books, the twinkly-eyed, super-charged Taoist continued, "Nettle tea is a great kidney boost. Kidney energy is linked with overall vitality if you have strong kidneys you'll live longer."

Find out more at:
www.superchargedTaoist.com & www.barefootdoctorglobal.com

Let There Be Light

Outdoor lighting used to be rather functional – security lights on the drive or the simply an 'outdoor light' above the front door. With a little thought lighting can add a big impact to your garden and enable it to be enjoyed into the summer and winter nights.

Most garden lighting is low voltage and will either run from a separate low voltage circuit or will incorporate a built in transformer. This type of lighting is simple to fit but always layout the entire system and put lights in preferred positions before fixing or burying cable.

High voltage lighting will need to be run off a 240v system requiring armoured cable and its therefore advisable to enlist the help of an electrician. If you opt for employing an electrician, get them to put in a couple of outdoor sockets too. They are more useful than you think!

Highlighting or 'uplighting' special features in the garden such as statuary or specimen trees will give your garden a 'theatrical feel' after dark. Use moveable, directional spotlights that have a spike to keep them secure in the ground and remember the higher the wattage the greater the amount of light. Downlighting works the same way but obviously floods light from above.

Solar powered lights have improved hugely over the years and are now an effective and easy to fit option for garden lighting. Most of them are charge by daylight rather than sunlight so will work even on cloudy or dark wintery days. The string lights are my absolute favourites and can be wound around virtually anything in the garden. Net lights are also really effective against walls and fences and of course can be used 'for life, not just Christmas!'

Are you on Facebook
or do you Tweet?

From Canopies to Compost

Known stateside as 'the fall', the autumn heralds both falling temperatures and falling leaves. The leafy, shade-providing canopies of summer will dramatically changing colour prior to parting with their annual hosts.

Canopies will become compost, as deciduous trees and shrubs prepare for the winter. To ensure winter survival, summer passengers will be discarded, leaving the familiar skeletal forms we associate with the colder months.

Customary leaf-fall is always preceded by an impressive burst of colour as the leaves dramatically change hues - almost a form of attention seeking in anticipation of their impending downfall.

During the spring and summer months, plants obtain their food as a result of photosynthesis. This process occurs in the green stems and leaves of the plant, and relies on the presence of chloroplasts. Chloroplasts are simply tiny bodies that contain the green chlorophyll pigments, the yellow-orange carotenoid pigments and other substances necessary for photosynthesis to occur. During the spring and summer chlorophyll pigments are more abundant than carotenoid pigments, resulting in a green leaf.

However, as the chlorophyll decomposes during the autumn, carotenoids become more dominant and provide the familiar golden hues. Some plants also produce and store red pigments during this stage and as these predominate the yellow carotenoids, the leaf will turn red. Subsequent leaf fall occurs as the tree or plant prepares for the harsh winter conditions.

If leaves were to be retained, freezing temperatures would turn the water contained in the plant cells to ice. These sharp, frozen particles would then expand and puncture the delicate cell membranes. This type of damage creates a breeding ground for bacteria and fungi rendering the tree susceptible to disease.

To prevent this scenario, leaves are discarded prior to the damaging frosts and the tiny scars covered with a protective seal. A new leaf will grow adjacent to this scar but never from the same site.

Sap stops flowing and vulnerable growing tips are safely encased in a tight, frost-resistant bud during the inclement months.

Leaf drop, or separation, is known as 'leaf abscission' and the crucial timing of this process is governed by the alteration of plant hormones. These are influenced by changes in temperature and light.

The relevant hormones weaken and eventually dissolve the 'glue' or pectin that adheres the leaves to the tree. Autumn winds then complete the traditional leaf-fall. A protective layer of cork guards against diseases entering through the leaf scars and also helps to prevent water loss.

Although leaves are discarded to avoid potential frost damage, some water must be retained in the trunk, branches and stems.

This is protected from freezing conditions by a rather ingenious form of plant 'antifreeze' that consists of a concentrated sugar solution and will prevent the formation of damaging ice particles in all but the harshest conditions.

A little water is also stored in the spaces between cells, away from the more delicate cell membranes.

These autumnal preparations are preventative measures. Known as 'cold-hardening', they occur at much the same time as you and I are looking for the hot water bottle.

Old Be-Leaf's

Even if you don't think of yourself as a gardener as such, autumn is a great time to get stuck in and have a go at clearing up and at the very least benefit from some outdoor exercise.

Leaf clearing will be in full swing and can be quite a drawn out process, depending on the frost or winds efforts in bringing the leaves down.

Don't be tempted to leave all your leaf clearing until the trees are bare and definitely not until the spring. A heavy wet blanket of fallen leaves will soon weaken and kill grass and plants underneath it and paths and steps can become dangerous when covered in wet leaves. Always keep fallen leaves out of ponds as when they rot they release gasses that can be harmful to the fish, and they will just 'gunk' up the pond. Putting netting, or a purpose-made wire netted frame, is the best way to catch the leaves and clear it off regularly. If the pond is too big for this method, endeavour to scoop as many leaves out as possible as often as possible.

It really is best to pick up leaves little and often and bag them up or put on the compost heap straight away. Mother Nature has a wicked sense of humour and will soon redistribute a pile of leaves which has been left 'for later'. If feasible try to get hold of a leaf blower or vacuum. They are actually quite reasonably priced now or it may be worth sharing the cost with a neighbour or friend. The little light electric versions are quite adequate (always use a circuit breaker) for most small gardens and there are terrific powerful, professional models for the larger garden, though these may be more cost effective to hire.

After spending years using a rake at this time of year, I always advocate using a machine as I have found:
a) it's easier and quicker but also
b) anything with an engine, and that makes a noise, is far more likely be commandeered by a fella!

If you have a rotary mower with a collection box, lift the blades and use it to collect the leaves, though not over gravel. And yes, I have seen it happen.

Leaving a few leaves in quiet places, like under a hedge or at the back of a shed or garage may encourage hedgehogs into your garden to hibernate.

I have actually seen a pile of leaves rise and fall with the gentle rhythmical snoring of a hibernating hedgehog. It's not a common experience and one well worth trying to encourage!

If using leaves for composting, remember that oak leaves take a lot longer to decompose than most others so try to keep them in a separate heap.

There are several 'accelerators' on the market (and of course the home made one, urine!) that can be mixed with your cache of leaves to speed up composting, particularly useful if bagging them.

It's worth doing, even if it seems a bit tedious; home-made leaf mould is great for the garden and is the mother of recycling.

Rocket Fuel

Rocket is easy to grow and a 'must-have' in the veg patch and kitchen. You will often have a surplus and a great way to utilise the older rocket leaves is to make a tasty dip.

Simply blend a large handful of leaves, 2 cloves of garlic and 50g of walnuts, then mix with the same volume of ricotta.

The added bonus is that it's delicious with courgettes which are also in plentiful supply at the same time.

Clever Cleavers

A sheep made out of strings of cleavers (Goosegrass) rolled into a ball and covered with the heads of cow parsley is an example of how you can be creative with your weeds!

The Firewood Rhyme

Beech wood fires are bright and clear
If the logs are kept a year
Chestnut only good they say
If for long it's laid away
Make a fire of elder tree
Death within your house will be
But ash new or ash old
Is fit for a Queen with a crown of gold
Birch and Fir logs burn too fast
Blaze up bright and do not last
It is by the Irish said
Hawthorn bakes the sweetest bread
Elmwood burns like churchyard mould
Even the very flames are cold
But ash green or ash brown
Is fit for a Queen with a golden crown
Poplar gives a bitter smoke
Fills your eyes and makes you choke
Apple wood will scent your room
With an incense-like perfume
Oaken logs, if dry and old
Keep away the winters cold
But ash wet or ash dry
A king shall warm his slippers by.

DIY Design

The dormant, winter months are a great time for a little Armchair Gardening and it's a good time to plan for the good gardening weather that lies ahead.

With everything naked and bare it's a great opportunity to review the basic structure and layout and plan changes and improvements that can be made. Whether it's just improving a particular area, introducing a patio, revamping a flowerbed or a complete overhaul, trust yourself to have a go at re-designing your own plot.

You don't have to be artistic or technical to create a plan. Simply make a rough sketch of what you already have – and you don't even have to let anyone else see it, so don't let your inhibitions hold you back.

Often, the best view point of the overall garden is from an upstairs window, (or sometimes even a neighbours upstairs window) so just sketch out a rough outline of your boundaries and include all beds, borders, paths, buildings, trees.

Also include manhole covers, drains, electricity poles and other fixed features that you will have to accommodate. Then, go outdoors and get a 'feel' for your garden.

This may sound a bit odd and always raises an eyebrow when I teach Garden Design courses but few people really know ALL the areas of their garden. There are always the out-of-bounds bits behind the shed and garage which have become a dumping ground; greenhouses may have become storage sheds; boundaries are often a bit of a grey area, overgrown and overlooked; and occasionally there are whole areas that are not used because of poor access or a lack of interest.

Make notes of things that irritate you and that you'd like to change but also the things that you really like.
Then go and put the kettle on.

This is a great bit ...
Make three lists. A list of all the things that you '*have*' to keep; include manholes, washing lines, sheds, trees and so on. The second list should be of '*would likes*'; would like to keep and would like to have. So include anything new that you would like to introduce into the garden ... within reason, as the last list is '*when I win the lottery*'. This last list isn't as frivolous as it sounds as any changes and alterations you make in the short term should always allow for larger changes that you may want to implement a few years down the line.

Also jot down a few points describing how you would like to use the garden or what you would like it to provide; a peaceful haven, a children's play area, a productive garden, low maintenance or maybe a mix of them all. You may think you know what you want but writing it down will help you focus on what you are trying to achieve overall.

Also list plants that you like – you don't have to know the Latin names or even be able to spell them properly, as long as you can describe them or get a picture of what you like. Be as specific as you can – colours, shapes, whether you want flowers to pick for the house or minimum maintenance shrubs. Don't forget ornaments, statues, benches and things like birdbaths and bird tables; and if you're brave, *that* water feature.

Treat yourself to a large sketch pad and a couple of coloured pencils and have some fun. Re-draw the boundaries and all the things that have to stay *and make several copies;* then start adding the things you'd like to introduce. Be creative and be brave. Use sweeping lines, curves, straight lines; be symmetrical and then be random; use as many pieces of paper as necessary and when you feel you've reached your 'creative peak', start to amalgamate all of your favourite ideas onto one sheet. As a new look develops, it will become clear that some projects can be done easily and with minimum cost or fuss and these can be tackled as you are able.

Once you start making changes, give some thought to incorporating lighting, outdoor power points and outdoor taps whilst the garden is under renovation. It may be that you need a little more assistance or advice before implementing these and larger projects but at least you will have a better idea of what you want and more importantly … what you don't want.

There's Only One Way to get rid of a mole …

There is probably nothing that strikes dread into the heart of a keen gardener more than a mole hill in the middle of their lawn.

Moles have a poor metabolism and have to eat their weight in food every day which means they have to travel extensively.   Since moles cannot put on body fat, they don't hibernate. Instead they spend the autumn preparing 'emergency' stores. Researchers have discovered 'larders' containing more than 1,000 stored earthworms.

There are many folklore-esque theories for getting rid of moles including using mothballs, milk bottles and little plastic windmills as deterrents.

The best method I have found is a castor oil and herb mix. Crush some dried rosemary leaves, chive, cloves, armetesia leaves, garlic and sage and add a couple of spoonfuls of castor oil. Add enough vodka, which will bring out the aromas and make it 'watery' enough to soak the rags in before putting them in the run.

My favourite advice on 'mole removal', was given to me by a tough old Welsh hill farmer, who swore it worked. You write a pleasant note to the mole asking him to move out of your garden or off your land as it is causing you distress, and put it down the 'mole hole'.

And finally a word of warning from another twinkly-eyed mole catcher, "Best not to kill your mole as you will attract all the other moles in the area into your garden - when they come to the funeral!"

Dance like no one is watching

Pig Tales

I couldn't compile this Allsortium without sharing my Pig Tales. Five years ago I decided to introduce a little pet pig to my Tiny Holding; I went all the way to the Lake District to fetch my little pig ... and came home with three – damn that nursery rhyme.

They were only the size of guinea pigs when I collected them and as it was a particularly frosty autumn, they spent their first three weeks in Wales snugly ensconced in my walk-in shower, complete with their straw bed.

A shed was cleared out for their next step toward facing the elements and they soon became a tourist attraction for local kids ... and adults. Pigs are incredibly social animals, often displaying far more social staying power than myself!

After a winter of much contentment, they were re-homed in a paddock behind the cottage which is when I discovered that the definition of a fence is 'something that pigs are the wrong side of'.

Pigs have a greater desire to be anywhere other than where they are supposed to be, than anything else I have ever known. I encountered more daily break outs than a teenagers back. At times it was challenging, even comical but at others, particularly after a hard day's work in the rain and cold, my sense of humour deserted me totally. It was a continual battle of wits and I felt more and more unarmed.

Suffice to say the installation of an electric fence eventually saw a truce being called.

With that challenge 'met', I subconsciously sought another ... I borrowed a small boar from quite simply the nicest pig breeder you will ever meet and who bizarrely happened to live less than a mile away, and whom I had overlooked in my initial search for pet pigs.

Owain had handed one of his little pet boars to Katie Price at her wedding to Alex, although after their separation the boar was returned to his Welsh roots – complete with pink nail varnish on his trotters!

So to ease his wounded pride, (the boar - not Owain's) we decided to put him in with my three girls. Only one was in season and, somewhat naively, I imagined he would forge some sort of lasting relationship with her which would also cheer him up and dissipate any rejection issues. He did indeed forge ahead ... with all three pigs. He was sent home.
A little too late.

To cut a long and fraught episode short(er), 5 months later and after spending numerous sleepless nights in the barn with all three pregnant piggies, I was the exhausted owner of 25 piglets.

Finding homes proved harder than initially expected, with negative press questioning the eventual size of 'small pet pigs', the recession biting and my own reluctance to let them go. But slowly and surely, the best pig homes were found and the numbers dwindled to twelve, which is how it stayed for the next 12 months.

The 'dirty dozen' developed quite a following, 'appearing' on Radio, in numerous columns and articles, blogging as Pig Brother, and three of them even graced events as the Olym-pigs – Mo Farrow, Usain Boar and Chris Hog. They provided much laughter, joy, pleasure and entertainment, woven with periods of exhaustion, worry and frustration. They gave much and took little; I adored them ... all.

As I re-homed the last two 'available' little piggies, I was reminded that it had been an incredible journey, through all types of emotional terrain. I was awash with relief and remorse in equal measures. I missed 'The Pig Pack' dreadfully.

I kept two – Frank who was a runt and who had to be neutered (I just felt that I owe him!) and his sister, Evil Edna, because she is evil and I wouldn't want to inflict her on anyone else.
After experiencing their loyalty, intelligence and uncomplicated take on life, I just couldn't be a pig-free zone again.

Frank and Edna returned, from their grass-let just up the road, to the Tiny Holding and as I let them back into the paddock 'where it all began', I allowed myself a sigh of reticent relief. I went to work reassuring myself, that everything was exactly as it was supposed to be. Although it had taken a while, all pigs had eventually found the most fabulous new homes and would bring much hap-pig-ness to their new families. I could concentrate on teaching Frank and Edna to walk in a harness and maybe even a few tricks.

All was well and, more importantly, manageable.

I got home later that day to find Frank and Edna had squeezed under the paddock fence and were busy annihilating the veg patch.

They say 'History has a habit of repeating itself.'

Despite the occasional frustrations caused by being outwitted by a pair of pigs, I still have the greatest respect and fondness for them as a species. So when I read about the opportunity to swim with pigs in the Bahamas I put it straight on my list of things to do and am working my way toward it.

Frank trying to convince me to take him swimming in the Bahamas.

Big Major Cay, also known as Pig Beach, is one of the 365 islands that make up the Exuma Cays. It is uninhabited, blessed with a natural water spring and is sheltered by a string of neighbouring islands that protects it from waves caused by tropical storms, all of which makes it the perfect piggy-playground for 25 or so resident pigs. It seems that nobody is sure how they got there. Some tales say that they survived a shipwreck and swam ashore, while others assert that sailors left them with the thought of coming back to eat them and forgot.

These sun-loving swine are smart enough to have learned that boats and people always have food and will, therefore, doggy paddle out to meet the visitors and lunch. Pigs are actually pretty good swimmers over short distance and appear to enjoy the water, especially when there is a free lunch involved.

Now, where did I put my passport?

The Piggin' Truth - Size Does Matter:
Despite the controversial 'hoo-ha' in the media about micro-pigs growing into 'big-pigs', my 'half-size hogs' are only knee height now they are fully grown which makes them much more manageable than the commercial pigs. Tea-cup pigs are hog-wash; the only fully grown pigs you will get that small are guinea pigs which are also the only type of pigs you should keep indoors (in my opinion). Part of the delight of having a pet pig is to be able to spend time with it out in the fresh air in its own environment.

DEFRA's own interpretation of a micro pig is a pig that has been bred over generations to be smaller in adulthood than most other species of pig.

My petite-pigs are also invaluable for a larger garden or allotment as they organically recycle all the waste growth and weeds that shouldn't really be put on the compost heap.

And I have grown the most 'hog-mongus' pumpkins and squashes on their little muck heap.

Pigs will also deter foxes, so my 'gang' have also been keeping my chickens safe and sound and I haven't had a visit from Foxy Loxy since having pigs.

It was Winston Churchill who noted, "dogs will look up to you; cats will look down on you but a pig will look you straight in the eye and see you as an equal."

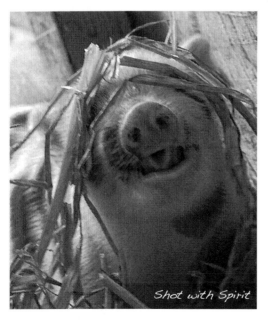

Shot with Spirit

Pigs are ranked No.4 in animal intelligence. Chimpanzees are ranked at the top together with the gorilla, orangutan, baboon, gibbon and monkey.

Dolphins and killer whales are ranked at no.2; elephants third and pigs fourth. They are easy to train and considered more intelligent than dogs.

Not known for their sporting abilities, you may be surprised to learn that a pig can run a 7-minute mile (though I don't think mine would ever be inclined to try) and they are also very good swimmers and prefer water to mud.

I have also learned that pigs don't like being picked up; they will absorb any amount of fuss, scratching and tummy rubbing but like to keep their trotters on the ground.

Connected to their dislike for being picked up, I have also learned that a pig's squeal can range from 110 to 115 decibels; a jet engine on take-off reaches about 112.

More Piggin' Amazing Facts ...

- The largest pig on record was a Poland China hog named Big Bill, who weighed 2,552 lbs
- The pig is rated the fourth most intelligent animal in the world but is mentioned only twice in the Bible
- Pigs will get restless and grunt loudly when high winds are on the way; it is believed they can see the wind!
- In France, it's illegal to name a pig Napoleon.

Hair and Snails

A salon in Tokyo is offering a new kind of beauty treatment – snail facials using a team of Japanese native snails. The snail bar with a difference puts the snails onto the client's face and leaves them to their own devices for 20 minutes or so. The molluscs' mucus is said to "remove dead skin, soothe any inflammation and help the skin retain moisture."

Whether the process actually does anything is a matter of debate among dermatologists, although snail mucus contains ingredients like hyaluronic acid and proteoglycans, which are already used in cosmetics and are known to promote tissue flexibility and skin healing.

And it seems the little shelled sloughers enjoy the 'slime-light' and are treated like celebrities themselves, as a spa attendant revealed, "These little snails are fed an allorganic diet of carrots, Japanese mustard spinach, and Swiss chard and are always kept in a room set to 20 degrees Celsius. Of the five inhouse snails, there are three "regulars" that are more frequently chosen for their superior mucusemitting ability."

And even if you wanted to 'shell' out a whopping $243 (£161) for a treatment, you'd have to wait in line. The beautifying powers of the snails are in high demand, and they're said to be fully booked for the next few weeks. But this is not the first time snails have been used in the beauty industry -there is already a cream called Elicina, which contains snails, available in the western market which hails from Chile and is produced in Portugal. It claims to help with stretch marks and sun spots; I wonder if it 'slows' the signs of aging!

And you can say what you like in front of a snail as they don't have ears but they do have a great sense of smell, which they use to locate food.

Aoccdrnig to a rscheearch at Cmabrigde Uinervtisy, it deosn't mttaer in waht oredr the ltteers in a wrod are witren, the olny iprmoatnt tihng is taht the frist and lsat ltteer be in the rghit pclae.

The rset can be a toatl mses and you can sitll raed it wouthit a porbelm.

Tihs is bcuseae the human mnid deos not raed ervey lteter by istlef, but the wrod as a wlohe. Celevr

Celebrity Chit-Chat with Christopher Biggins

Renowned for being the country's Top Dame, Christopher Biggins loves being busy and also enjoys being outdoors. He told me, "I enjoy being outdoors and in my garden but it's often just impossible in this British weather. When I went to the Hampton Court Flower Show Opening Night earlier this year, the rain simply pounded down, although we still had a wonderful time.

He admitted to picking up tips from the RHS Shows, "I like to see the flowerbeds and emulate them.

"Our own garden is like an extension of our dining room with a lovely table and chairs and beautiful flowers.

"It's a very pretty town garden and we have a wonderful girl who comes in to help. We just tell her what we'd like. I love all types of country flowers in the garden but we always have white orchids, the stephanotis in the house.

"We live in Hackney, near Columbia Road market so we often go and collect the most beautiful cut flowers." He explained. "If I lived in the country I'd definitely grow vegetables but they take up too much room in a town garden.

"I remember one of my relatives having an allotment when I was young and friends in London now have one too; it seems people visit their allotment on a Sunday morning and then stagger home a little drunk in time for Sunday lunch. Allotments are great things."

Ironically, the Greek translation of Christopher's favourite indoor flowers stephanotis, means 'crown' and he was crowned King ('or Queen', he laughed) of the Jungle for I'm a Celebrity Get Me Out Of Here in 2010, the delightful Dame admitted, "I found the Jungle very difficult indeed. I have a three line whip;

"I loved every minute of it;
I would not have missed it for the world
and I would never do it again.

"As viewers you only see one hour of twenty four, it's very boring although I did thoroughly enjoy being outdoors. I've always hated camping and as a kid remember waking up in a caravan in the middle of a field covered in dew; I'm much more of a Four-Seasons Hotel man these days. I thought I would be worried about creepy crawlies in the jungle but I had the best sleep ever. The air was wonderful."

www.christopherbiggins.com

Zen Hens

It has been proven that happy and healthy chickens produce the deepest yellow or orangey egg yolks.

And whilst a nice, relaxing, free-range life style is one of the best ways to ensure happy hens, there are also a couple of natural tonics that will keep hens healthy too.

Chick weed is one of the best natural tonics for chickens (hence the name) and is a great treat for hens. Pick it fresh and give them a handful whenever you can, they will love it. Perhaps a little easier to provide regularly though is spirulina which is an excellent tonic for chickens and, in fact, all birds. Spirulina can also benefit dogs – when a dog drinks from a muddy puddle rather than a clean drinking bowl, it is often because it is requiring the algae. It's also great for humans – spirulina, not drinking out of muddy puddles!

One of the oldest life forms on Earth, spirulina is a blue-green micro-algae, often described as the original 'superfood.' It is so nutrient dense that you could survive on it and water alone and is the richest and most easily digested source of protein on the planet.

As a tonic for chickens, simply mix a little spirulina powder with water and put in their run alongside ordinary clean drinking water; they will choose the algae if they need it, as will a dog.

Always make sure it is offered purely as an option, so don't add to food or make it their only water source.

For us, the powder or flakes can be added to food or smoothies or the pill form can be taken as a supplement. The list of benefits is a long one, including increased energy, improved clarity, boosted immune system and it can even promote weight loss.

Eggs-traordinary Facts:

Eggs have a natural coating called a "bloom" that protects the eggs and keeps them fresh for a week or two. Don't be tempted to wash your fresh eggs as the shells are porous and will absorb the smells around them and anything on them.

And I have discovered that there are actually benefits of having egg on your face as the membrane of an egg makes a refreshing undereye mask. After you've cracked open your egg, carefully peel off the membrane that coats the insides, apply right under your eyes and let it dry before gently washing off.

Egg whites also make a great face mask, cleaning out and tightening pores naturally. Soak strips of paper towel in whipped egg whites. Place the paper towel strips to your face, let them dry and then peel them off. Rinse well with warm water and then splash with cold water.

Use the yolks to make a nourishing hair conditioner; whip up one or two yolks, depending on the length of your hair, and add just a touch of heated, liquid coconut oil until you have a creamy mixture. You can use olive oil, but coconut oil leaves your hair smelling better and a little less like mayonnaise.

Apply the mixture to damp hair and leave on for 10 minutes. Rinse your hair very, very well with cool water (do NOT use hot water, or you'll end up with scrambled eggs). Then shampoo out the rest, still using only warm water.

And finally the eggshells themselves can also be used to powder your face. Wash your empty eggshells thoroughly and leave to dry well on a radiator or in the sun. Then simply grind in a mortar and pestle until you get a fine powder. It's a very translucent powder that won't colour your face at all but will reduce 'shine'.

Hen Party!

I want to be 'a Lawn'

As spring arrives, you may think your lawn has turned into moss through the winter months. It is actually known as winter moss and, as the name suggests, it thrives on wintery conditions.

The good news is that when the weather dries up and warms up the moss will disappear - but don't be fooled, it will have sown its spores and be back with a vengeance next year. If feasible, it is better to tackle the problem than ignore it. Start by 'scarifying' to remove the old thatch and moss. We always use a petrol driven machine (which you can hire) but the electric versions are okay (always use a circuit breaker) and even a springbok rake will do the trick on a small area. If you do hire a machine, then maybe sharing it (and the cost) with a neighbour or friend may help.

Don't be too enthusiastic. Even though the scarifier won't remove grass, if you haven't done this treatment for a while the results can be quite dramatic as you watch your lawn disappearing into the collection bag.

Scarifying in the autumn is also beneficial, though once each way should be enough. Over-sow with a good utility seed mix that doesn't contain rye and brush in if necessary.

'Spiking' compacted areas of the lawn is always worthwhile as it allows water and air to penetrate the soil surface and will encourage healthy grass growth. It may not be necessary to do the whole lawn – just worn areas in front of kid's football goals or tracks that have been worn by foot (or paw) fall.

Mowing regularly (not just when you are nagged) is also beneficial to encourage the lower side shoots to grow out horizontally to provide dense ground cover and limit weed invasion.

Feeding your lawn is also beneficial. I know people shy away from it as they think they'll have to mow more often but it is important for a good-looking and healthy lawn.

Each time you mow you are removing a part of the 'plant' that makes its food – a bit like depleting the store cupboard!

I have always said you should never be a slave to the lawn but being a friend will help!

Put your heart into it ...

Watch the Birdie

Over half of the UK population feed their garden birds. It's a great way to help the birds overcome shortages in their natural food and cope with severe weather conditions, as well as encouraging them into the garden for us to watch and appreciate. It's important, however, that feeding is done responsibly and with commitment as the birds soon come to rely on a regular source of supplemented food. It is also important to manage your garden well, in order for the birds to obtain a range of more natural and nutritious foodstuff from flowerbeds, lawns and shrubberies.

There is a wide range of bird food on the shelves to choose from and different dishes will attract different birds. As is often the case, the more expensive food is better for the birds, as cheaper mixes are often padded out with barley and wheat grains which will attract pigeons, doves and pheasants and deter the smaller species. Other economy brands use crushed dog biscuits for bulk, which should only be fed to birds if soaked.

Household scraps can be an inexpensive way to encourage birds into the garden; Robins and wrens love mild grated cheese, cold baked potatoes (opened up) and mash is always appreciated. Dried fruit, sultanas, raisins and currants appeal to robins, thrushes and tits as does fresh fruit like apples, pears. Pastry, cooked or uncooked, is a real treat if made with proper fats and suet will attract woodpeckers as well as smaller birds.

Avoid putting out salty food, which usually includes bacon and bacon rind and remember there is no nutritional value in bread, it's just a filler.

And don't give your feathered friends anything mouldy or stale. Stale food allows salmonella bacteria to breed which can be fatal to some species and some moulds can cause respiratory infections.

Come Dine With Me

Not all birds will feed from a table. Thrushes and dunnocks, for example prefer to feed from the ground, (obviously not a good idea if you have feline visitors). Siskins, sparrows and tits will enjoy hanging seed and nut feeders. Be creative and put suet and fat into crevices in a fence post or sawn log to attract tree creepers and nut hatches and spread out feeders to avoid feathered-fights!

Mesh bags should be avoided as they can trap a bird by its foot, or even beak, and always keep the feeding stations clean and free from old stale food.

Gardening Groan

Botanists have found a vegetable that cleans your teeth when you eat it – it's called a 'bristle sprout'!

Celebrity Chit-Chat with BBC's Bill Turnbull

BBC Breakfast presenter and author of the Bad Bee Keeper's Club, Bill Turnbull is in his 14th season as a 'bad Bee keeper'. He explained, "I started keeping bees 13 years ago after a swarm turned up at the bottom of my garden. I called the Police, and they called a bee keeper who just came along and collected the swarm in a cardboard box. I was so inspired and wanted to see if I had that Zen-like ability to do the same."

"There's only one thing better than collecting a swarm and that's when one re-houses itself. I have a bait hive on top of my garage roof and have had two swarms use it this year. The second swarm weren't even my bees, which is even better!"

Enjoying time spent outdoors, Bill described himself as being "better with husbandry than horticulture," and explained, "I'm not a gardener; we have a half acre plot and I mow the lawn with great reluctance, my wife does all the rest. My father always said I couldn't tell a cabbage from a rose and he's right. I grew up on a small-holding with hens, geese, sheep, pigs and heifers and I think that's rubbed off on me. As well as my bees, I keep chickens and have two black labs, Nina and Bonny. Nina is bee-phobic," he added, "she got stung once and now prefers to wait by the car whilst I check my bees."

And Nina is not the only Turnbull to have been stung. "I've been stung more times than I can remember," laughed Bill, "though over the years I am actually being stung less.

I don't inspect the bees quite so often now, although recently I did do something quite stupid even by my standards. When returning from holiday I thought I'd just take the roof off one of the hives to see what was going on and a bee flew straight up and stung me on the nose. It wasn't pretty and the swelling is a bit awkward for my TV work."

Ever the pragmatist he added, "I wouldn't not want to get stung, it would make bee keeping too easy and then everyone would be doing it."

He continued to describe his enchantment with the little insects. "I find bees amazing creatures, intricate and beautiful. Each hive is a little city, with its own issues and problems. Every time you open the hive, you have a series of questions to ask, it's like solving a puzzle every time. I find it clears my mind of other things."

As an external examiner for the Centre for Journalism Studies at Cardiff University, Bill still enjoys visiting the city. "I was actually a student at Cardiff University myself and my wife worked in Cardiff for years too. We both enjoy coming back to the city, it's a great place, as is the rest of Wales. I'm also Patron for Bees for Development an independent organisation which is based in Monmouth but I've not visited them yet. I once ran the London Marathon dressed as a bee keeper, to raise money for them and I vowed it was the last marathon I'll ever run; in a bee suit or otherwise." Bill still uses his treadmill every day though, "It's part of my sleep management regime," he explained, "After doing the Breakfast Show, I have to go home and sleep, or I become a basket case. But then I need to do something in the afternoon to tire me enough to sleep at night."

The well-liked presenter is slightly bemused at the success of his book, which is going from strength to strength, "An American publisher has recently released it in the States, renaming it, Confessions of a Bad Bee Keeper. I'm going over to do a Tour of the North East at the end of the month, and most of the book signings are at bee keeping conventions. It's ironic really as the book wasn't written for experienced bee keepers but for just for people interested to know a bit about bee keeping."

What the Buzz is About ...

I began keeping bees five years ago. It's addictive. I was extremely fortunate to find a fabulous local bee-keeper, Alan, who has probably forgotten more than I will ever know and who kindly and patiently mentored me through my first season. I also did a bee-keeping course but only after having twelve months of hands-on experience. Most people, it transpires, do a course before getting their bees which is probably the most sensible way (I've never let that stop me). I will never forget the enormity of looking down into a full hive of about 6,000 bees for the first time, knowing there was only a thin veil between them and my face.

It's not for everyone, as I wrote for one publication last year:

"Bee keeping is not just about having a 'box of bees' at the bottom of the garden. Taking care of bees will provide the most amazing feelings of satisfaction and pride but they can also deal some of the most confidence-squashing disappointments too; add a good scoop of frustration and a pinch of bewilderment and, as far as I can tell so far, you have 'Bee Keeping."

And don't worry if you don't actually fancy keeping bees yourself, there are still ways that you can contribute to the world of the honey bee, as well as other bees and wildlife, without such commitment.

There are many plants that will encourage bees and other insects into your garden (or even onto a balcony) throughout the year. Here are a few suggestions: Angelica, aster, buddleia, cardoon, cornflower, dahlia (single-flowered), bluebell, bugle, crab apple, daffodil, flowering cherry and currant, forget-me-not, hawthorn, hellebore, borage, wallflower, clover, primrose, pulmonaria, pussy willow, rhododendron, rosemary, viburnum, thrift. delphinium, eryngium, fuchsia, globe thistle, heather, ivy, lavender, penstemon, scabious, sedum, Verbena bonariensis, golden rod, aquilegia, astilbe, campanula, comfrey, everlasting sweet, fennel, foxglove, geranium, potentilla, snapdragon, stachys, teasel, thyme, verbascum, chamomile, runner beans and peas.

Remember that whist a wildlife garden shouldn't be a neglected garden, the good news is that wildlife doesn't like your garden to be too neat either; dandelions, daisies, clover and celandines are all adored by bees and other wildlife.

Bees and other insects will also appreciate a regular supply of water, though not necessarily clean water! A bog garden (or even a tray of wet soil & compost) makes an ideal drinking spot for bees and butterflies as they can land and remove water from the soil without fear of drowning. A bog garden will also provide the perfect drinking hole for butterflies and dragonflies.

You can also 'bee-friendly' in other ways ...

- Plant flowering hedgerows as boundaries instead of evergreen varieties or even wooden panels. Even mixing flowering varieties and evergreens will help. Flowering hedges can also be planted in front of wooden fences.
- Plant fruit trees; the bees will benefit from the blossom and you'll benefit from the fruit use ground cover plants, like ground-hugging thyme and pulmonaria, instead of bark mulches.
- Use herbs and low growing bee-friendly plants for containerised displays instead of traditional summer bedding.
- Plant low growing herbs like thyme and chamomile through your lawn. They will also give off the most delicious fragrance as you walk on or cut the grass.
- Use roof spaces for bee-friendly plants. Living roofs are a fabulous way to encourage wildlife into your garden.
- 'Bee pro-active' and encourage others to be nice and befriend bees and wildlife too.

- Join a Bee Keeper's Association – you don't have to be a bee keeper.
- If you have space for hives, offer it to a bee keeper to keep a hive or two; you can benefit from pollination, observation and a jar or two of honey!

Bees prefer the same variety of plants to be planted in large 'drifts' or groups as it not only makes it easier for them to locate but it is also easier for them to collect the nectar and pollen from one area rather than having to visit several sites. Useful places for more 'bee-search':

- British Bee Keeper's Association   www.bbka.org.uk
- Welsh Bee Keeper's Association   www.wbka.com
- Gwent Bee Keeper's Association   www.gbka.co.uk
  (I am a member of GBKA, hence their inclusion!)
- www.vanishingbees.com
- www.beedata.com
- www.nationalbeeunit.com
- www.beesfordevelopment.org
- www.biobees.com

Revive tired bees with a little drop of honey.

Perfect Plants for Pollinators

You don't have to keep bees to help them out. As I've mentioned, simply include as many 'plants for pollinators' in your garden to keep them well fed! Here's a comprehensive list.

Perfect for Pollinators Plant List:

Winter   Nov – Feb
Crocus biflorus (crocus)
Eranthis hyemalis (winter aconite)
Galanthius nivalis (snowdrops – single flower forms)
Helleborus x hybridus (hellebores)
Lonicera x purpusii (honeysuckle)
Mahonia x media (Oregan grape)
Salix aegyptiaca (willow)
Sarcococca hookeriana (winter box)

Spring   Mar – May
Acer campestre (field maple)
Acer pseudoplantanus (sycamore)
Aesculus hippocasstanum (horse chestnut)
Ajuga reptans (bugle)
Berberis darwinii (Darwin's barberry)
Caltha palustris (marsh marigold)
Chaenomeles japonica (Japanese quince)
Crataegus monogyna (hawthorn)
Crocus spp & cultivars (various crocus)
Euphorbia amygdaloides (wood spurge)

Geum rivale (water avens)
Hebe spp & cultivars (various hebe)
Ilex aquifolium (holly)
Lunaria annua (honesty)
Malus 'John Downie' (crab apple)
Mespilus germanica (medlar)
Primula vulgaris (primrose)
Ribe nigrum (blackcurrant)
Salix lanata (woolly willow)
Taraxacum officinale (dandelion)

Summer   June- Aug
Achillea millefolium (common Yarrow)
Allium schoenoprasum (chives)
Aquligia spp (columbine/Granny's Bonnet)
Buddleja davidii (butterfly bush)
Calamintha nepeta spp (catmint)
Centaurea nigra (hard head knapweed)
Clematis vitalba (Old man's Beard)
Dahlia (open centred forms)
Digitalis purpurea (foxglove)
Echinacea purpurea (coneflower)
Fuchsia magellanica (hardy fuchsia)
Geum 'Borisii' (geum)
Helianthus annuus (sunflower – single flowered forms)
Jasminum officinale (common jasmine)
Lavendula angustifolia (English lavender)
Mentha spicata (garden mint)
Potentilla fruiticosa (shrubby potentilla)
Rosminarus officinalis (rosemary)

Sedum spectabile (ice plant)
Tamarix ramosissima (tamerisk)
Tetradium daniellii (bee bee tree)
Thymus spp & cultivars (thyme)
Tillia x europea (common lime)
Verbascum olympicum (verbascum)
Vicia faba (broad bean)
Zinnia elegans (zinnia – open centred forms)

Autumn   Sept – Oct
Anemone hupehensis (Japanese anemone)
Aster amellus (perennial aster)
Aster novi-belgii (Michaelmas daisy)
Chrsnathemum cultivars (open flower forms)
Crocus speciosus (autumn-flowering crocus)
Hedera helix (common ivy)
Tillia henryana (late flowering lime tree)

Whacky Weather

In 1855 and 1879 intense frosts in the UK were severe
enough to kill mature trees and The Times reported, "large
numbers of work people are suffering immensely through
enforced idleness." Whilst on the 3rd December 1948
Hawarden Bridge in North Wales recorded temperatures of
almost 17 degrees.

Snow Joke

I thought I had discovered a snowman's mass grave but then I remembered it's where I sowed the carrots!

Top Tip

Use a petrol leaf blower to blow soft, fresh snow from paths and driveways.

Great Balls of Ice

During frosty weather, fill balloons with water coloured with a little food dye and put outside to freeze. Once frozen, cut off the balloon for some amazing funky coloured iced shapes.

The most affectionate thing in the world is a wet and muddy dog

Celebrity Chit-Chat **with Bill Bailey**

Comedian, musician and actor Bill Bailey agrees with me when I claim that one of the biggest accolades is to have a plant named after you.

He told me, "I was thrilled to have a Pitcher Plant named after me a couple of years ago. Borneo Exotics, who are a highly regarded breeder of Nepenthes, got to hear about the work I do in Sumatra with the Orangutans and for other Indonesian Charities and they named a hybrid cultivar from Sumatra, which is crossed with a Filipino one, Nepenthes 'Bill Bailey' in recognition of my work. It's a great honour to be revered in plant form especially a carnivorous one rather than a dahlia."

Well known as a regular guest on QI and Never Mind the Buzzcocks, Bill adores the outdoors and has presented numerous animal and wildlife programmes including Bill Bailey's Bird Watching Bonanza. He recalled, "One of the greatest moments was when a woman told me that her 13 yr old son who was addicted to his X Box, asked for a pair of binoculars to watch the birds with after watching one of my programmes. I've noticed that kids love to know the names of things; it gives them a sort of power."

Despite his obvious knowledge and appreciation of plants, Bill confessed, "My wife Kristin, is the real gardener in our organisation. I just know the things I like; like the scent of the Clerodendrum which is just intoxicating on a summer evening. We turned our London garden into a sandy beach, so it's low maintenance as I'm away a lot. We had it landscaped with white sand, tropical plants and a pond with Gunnera and lilies. I work from a studio in the garden so it's good to have year round interest outside."

www.billbailey.com

Animal Communication

In Rupert Sheldrake's captivating book, 'Dogs That Know When Their Owners Are Coming Home' he shares his research into how animals and people communicate telepathically. He told me, "60% of dogs get it right and 30% of cats. I don't believe that cats are less intelligent just less interested."

Rupert has also carried out numerous other experiments with telepathy. "I believe anyone can communicate telepathically, however every human ability differs, so some people will be more sensitive to telepathy than others. There are several tests on my website where people can test their abilities. The results are above chance."

"I have always been preoccupied with living things. Being outdoors is very important to me. I walk on Hampstead Heath every day and love the feeling of being outdoors. And I love walking in Wales. The Wye Valley is particularly beautiful. My own London garden is too small and shady to grow my own vegetables although I do grow tomatoes and chillies. I love ferns and also grow a lot of flowers. I would definitely grow more if I had the space.

"Most of nature is inherently chaotic. It's not rigidly determined in the old sense. It's not rigidly predictable."

– Rupert Sheldrake

www.rupertsheldrake.com

Paws for Thought

A little ironically, when I first started communicating with animals, I kept quiet about it. But as my confidence has grown and my concern about what other people think has diminished, I have talked more and more openly about it. Sharing experiences with Rupert Sheldrake also helped!

Whilst each interaction is a rather magical experience, there is nothing exclusive about it; anyone can do it. Like most things the first thing to do is to get out of your own way.

If you have a pet, or work with animals in any capacity, you will at some stage have talked to them. It may well only be, "C'mon, let's go for a walk", or "Move over," in the stable but let's face it, often it's a lot more. Communicating is just adding the art of listening. Instead of doing all the talking, take time to listen to the animal. You may not hear anything, you may 'feel' something or even 'see' a response; remember this isn't Disney, you are not suddenly going to get your dog discussing the economic climate with you in a Stephen Fry kind of voice. 'Thankfully', some would say. Just the same as human to human communication is learned and taken to the level you choose, so it is the same with animal communication.

There is no secret but the following suggestion may help you to get started ...
Choose somewhere quiet and with little external distraction for either of you. Then out loud or in your head, explain what you are doing to your animal or pet.

It may sound something like this: "Yogi, I have been reading about communicating with animals and apparently everyone can do it. I thought I could try with you. It may mean that I can understand you better and of course you could let me know what makes you happy and what you need. Would you like that? Shall we have a go?"

And then just listen. You will inevitably 'get' a response; trust it, you are communicating. It may not be the response you want. A friend rang me in tears to say she had said just what I recommended and had immediately heard, "No!". She was actually upset by the fact she thought she couldn't do it until I pointed out she had heard 'No'; it wasn't what she wanted to hear but it was a start, she was communicating with her cat.

There are a few points I have learned. Every animal has a very different personality - some will be keen to chat, some will be shy, some off hand and some quite demanding. Some will be smarter than others. But most animals will answer you literally. If I ask an animal to communicate and then finish with, "What do you think?" I will often get, "About food". When asked how can their lives be improved, most dogs will reply, 'more food and more walks'. Most cats will reply, "more peace and quiet."

Tortoises tend to speak slowly and deliberately and hamsters very quickly and without punctuation.

It is what you would expect but don't let that spoil your

experience by thinking you are 'making it up'. The more practice you can put in the more rewarding it becomes.
I have had incredibly enlightening conversations with animals that have been of benefit to me personally but also being able to share an animal's fears or frustrations with their owner obviously benefits their relationship.

I have heard that being able to communicate with animals is a gift but I believe the gift is what they can teach us.

Talk to the paw!

Animal Magic

I am highly honoured to be an Ambassador for World Animal Day. Celebrated on 4th October, we encourage you to get involved and do something special for the animals.

MISSION STATEMENT for WORLD ANIMAL DAY:
- To celebrate animal life in all its forms
- To celebrate humankind's relationship with the animal kingdom
- To acknowledge the diverse roles that animals play in our lives – from being our companions, supporting and helping us, to bringing a sense of wonder into our lives
- To acknowledge and be thankful for the way in which animals enrich our lives

To find out how you can help *www.worldanimalday.org.uk*

Daft as a Bat?

Some plants attract night flying insects that in turn encourage bats into the garden. 'Bat attractors' include cornflower, phlox, evening primrose, spearmint, salvia and stocks. I remember Mum finding bats in our attic when we were kids and so she had to phone the SNCO (Statutory Nature Conservation Organisation) so they could visit the site. She left a note for Dad saying, "Batman calling this afternoon!"

And Robin ...

The Robin is one of the few birds to sing on Christmas Day; their beautiful song is how they mark out the boundaries of their territory and they hold that territory all year.

Love These Wise Words ...

Taken from Lao Tzu in the Tao Te Ching:
"Stretching herself too thin,
she breaks her connections;
staying to busy, she has no time;
defining herself through others,
she loses her own definition.
The Wise Woman waters her own garden first."

At the end of the day your nose should be dirty, your hair messy and your eyes shining.

Celebrity Chit-Chat with James Wong

Making plants and weeds seem trendy is easy for the presenter of the TV series 'Grow Your Own Drugs', James Wong. "I grew up in Malaysia and Singapore where there is a different attitude to plants than you have in the UK," he explained. Friends from the UK were just not as excited about them. I think it's because often their first introduction to horticulture is a boring trip to a nursery to pick up a few trays of bedding plants, a bit like carpet samples." He continues, "In Asia, plants are not just used like soft furnishing, they're also useful and provide solutions for everyday problems. They had to have a function to have a place in the garden; we say they have to be good to eat or treat." he continued passionately.

The ethno botanist (a scientist who studies plants and their uses) admitted that the remedies he creates are not strictly his own. "I just put a bit of a twist on a long standing recipe," he explained modestly. "It is well known that peppermint and fennel seeds relieve trapped wind for example. I have used those herbs to make sugar mice which is a much nicer way to take the medicine. They are quick and simple to make, only have 4 ingredients and are a good way to deal with too many sprouts. I have also created a very trendy cocktail for indigestion," he adds, "It tastes really good and would be at home in any Cocktail bar; I'm very proud of it.

"Most weed species are medicinal, I did a lot of research in Ecuador and was surprised to find out that they favour the introduced European species like dandelion, plantain and nettles. People still think that medicinal plants are exotic and can only be found up the Amazon but most people will have the basic species in their lawn, and if you are a lazy gardener, they will also be organic."

A regular guest presenter on BBC's Country File, James continues to share his plant knowledge. "There are very few plants with no recorded use. I've never eaten Holly for example but it has spiritual and ornamental qualities as secondary uses.

"My favourite plant is probably lavender," he admitted when asked, "it's not considered very cool or trendy but it has so many uses, from easing anxiety to calming a rash. And in the 19th century it was popular as a culinary herb, like sage and parsley, though it has an unusual taste."

What's the green fingered guru's own garden like? "It's fallen by the wayside a bit lately as I've been busy filming, it has lots of tropical effect plants that remind me of Singapore. The really funny thing is that as growing up in the tropics, everyone wants the traditional English Gardens with the nice lawn, snapdragons and bulbs in the borders. Mum is actually from Newport in South Wales and when I used to come and visit her I would always take back lots of bulbs and cottage garden type plants. They never did very well in the heat though," he admitted, adding enthusiastically, "People still pick up a little bit of my Welsh accent occasionally," he laughed, "I like that, it makes me feel very cosmopolitan."

www.jameswong.co.uk

Mint idea ...

Rubbing mint leaves into your skin will keep midges and mosquitoes away. Oh, and mosquitoes have 47 teeth and are particularly attracted to the colour blue.

Feeling Sporely?

I get asked a lot by keen gardeners if I have a way of dealing with hay fever. The debilitating condition is a rhinitis allergy wherein the mucus membranes of the nose and sinus areas become inflamed and is associated with the spring and summer pollens. However, in our damp British climate, the pollen season extends into the mold spore season with the same debilitating effects felt by allergy sufferers.

Mold spores are seeds of molds and fungi. Outdoor mold spores grow in moist shady areas, such as soil, decaying leaves, compost piles, and rotting wood and spore counts are higher when it rains or when the weather is very humid. Some are released in dry, windy conditions, while other spores are released in high humidity when there is fog and dew. Unfortunately fallen autumn leaves provide a favourite environment for the spores and allergic conditions often worsen when walking through or raking fallen autumn leaves.

You cannot prevent an allergic reaction to fungal spores but you can often alleviate the symptoms by taking a daily dose of vitamin C. There are also many herbs you can take to lessen the symptoms of allergies to mold. Each herb has its own function, to help with congestion, try taking Burdock. Marshmallow root is great to help get rid of mucous and goldenseal root acts as a bacterial product and will also soothe inflamed membranes.

Or try smearing a little Vaseline inside each nostril, as the pollen and spores are then prevented from irritating the nasal passages.

Some people will always stare.
Make it worth their while.

The Tree Zodiac

Much gratitude and respect to Graham Phillips for allowing me to share his Tree Zodiac. You can read more about Graham at www.grahamphillips.net.

The stars of the zodiac that we now see as constellations such as Virgo, Aquarius and so on were seen by the ancient Celts to form the images of trees.

As there were thirty-two of these constellations, and not twelve as there are now, the patterns that the Celts saw in the stars was very different than those familiar today.

This does not mean that the stars were different, rather that they saw the same stars to form different designs in the night sky – usually the shape of leaf of the relevant tree. Just like the modern zodiac, this tree zodiac was thought to influence the personality and characteristics of a person born in a particular sign.

However, until now, no writings have been found to provide specific details concerning the characteristics thought to be possessed by people born in each tree birth sign.

As an interesting exercise, Graham has attempted to reconstruct these ancient tree signs. From computer analysis of a selection of volunteers who completed a detailed questionnaire about themselves, he has determined certain personality traits that appear to be shared by those born in each sign.

21 – 31 December   Holly

As holly berries remain on the tree all winter long, they are a much-needed food source for birds. Also, as holly was the only large-leafed evergreen tree native to northwest Europe, it was firmly associated with winter survival.

Those born in the Holly sign can modify and adapt their behaviour to suit their present company and current predicament. The Holly person is forever challenging the world around them. They possess a mischievous quality that sometimes bewilders those about them and few but the most perceptive will know the Holly's true intentions. They also have the capacity to grasp the root of a problem, possessing shrewd insight into the true cause of difficulties they encounter. Holly people are forthright and astute; they have inquiring and probing minds and are remarkably self-disciplined. They can, however, have an eccentric side to their nature that some people find disturbing

1 – 10 January   Spruce

Like the holly and the ivy, the tough and adaptable spruce is still associated with midwinter celebration as the Christmas tree.

Those born in the Spruce sign are usually optimistic concerning their chosen ventures and a strong sense of intuition often brings them much success. Outwardly the Spruce is humorous, witty and fun-loving, but inwardly they maintain a serious, sharp-eyed attitude to life. They are ambitious, with the capacity to exercise authority, while a strong will and conscientious attitude results in many Spruce people holding positions of responsibility. They do, however, tend to have a nasty temper and are sometimes quick to take offence.

11 – 20 January   Ivy

Although ivy is not a tree in the botanical sense, the ancient Celts regarded it as one. Its black berries that ripen early in the year were considered a promise that nature was only sleeping and would again awake.

Those born in the Ivy sign are natural performers, excellent entertainers and at ease in most company. They love to surround their lives with excitement and can adapt their character and humour to suit the occasion. Ivy people will fascinate those around them and are always prepared to be the centre of attention. Not only are Ivy people learned and knowledgeable on so many subjects, they will discuss anything in an enlightening and entertaining manner. Sometimes, though, their outgoing ways can be too much for calmer people to handle.

21 - 31 January   Pine

As the most abundant evergreen tree, the pine represented a successful passage through winter. It was associated with the horned-god Cernonus, as pine forests were a habitat for his sacred animal, the red deer.

Those born in the sign of the Pine have considerable powers of concentration, coupled with diverse technical and artistic skills. They are extremely self-disciplined, possessing the mental stamina to remain on top of most situations. The Pine person is a great conversationalist and an eager listener. They will take a central role in social activities, and in business matters are usually successful. The Pine person is usually good with money, but a thrifty disposition can sometimes make them tight-fisted

1 – 11 February   Hazel

As new shoots regularly replace hazel stems, making it appear forever young, it was a tree closely linked with youth and innocence.

The Hazel person has tremendous creative potential and once their true vocation is realized success is virtually guaranteed. Often, however, they are too self-conscious of their failures and ignore their achievements. Hazels are true romantics and love to fantasize and reminisce. Many share a marvelous talent to captivate an audience, enlivening conversation by their sheer enthusiasm for romance and adventure. Hazels are natural performers and a flamboyant, dramatic personality never fails to win friends and gain influence. Those born in this sign can often retain a youthful personality and appearance throughout most of their lives.

12 – 22 February   Alder

As the alder is found in wetlands it is often surrounded by morning mist. It thus became associated with the Celtic water spirit known as The Lady of the Lake in the Arthurian legend, and known as the Lady Tree. A cheerful temperament makes most relationships easy for those born in the Alder sign and many enjoy considerable popularity. Business capacity is well above average, although partners or colleagues are required to help with sound administration and investments.

Most born in this cycle have a deep sense of responsibility, generally sharing a conscientious and principled attitude to life. Alder people are warm, loving and caring but tend to have an idealistic view of life. Trustworthy and honest, they expect others to be the same.

23 February - 7 March   Sallow
As it grows in river valleys, like the alder, the Sallow too was also regarded as sacred to the Lady of the Lake.

Those born in the Sallow sign have wonderful humility and are seldom, if ever, arrogant or vain. Admirable though these qualities are, they may result in too much self-sacrifice and a lack of consideration for their own essential needs. Those born in this sign should make a determined effort not to let acquaintances walk all over them. Sallow people are sometimes too kind and generous for their own good. This is also a sign of considerable creativity and an affinity with nature. Many people with deep insight are born during this cycle.

8 – 20 March   Ash
Those born in the Ash sign are romantic and affectionate, although sometimes a little too sentimental. They are open

and giving and willingly offer their trust.

They allow themselves to be captivated by those who bring adventure to their lives, providing it is not too disruptive. For the Ash to be at their best, they need a stable partner who has a responsible attitude to life. Ash people have a strong affinity with nature and are usually extremely fond of animals. Many vegetarians are born in this sign.

21 - 31 March   Apple
Most born in the Apple sign are sprightly and quick-witted, and many share a strong compulsion to keep on the move. Curious by nature, they show considerable interest in the affairs of their friends, and are ever ready to help or intercede on behalf of others.

They are perhaps the most inquisitive of any sign. The Apple person just hates to feel excluded. However, they are not natural followers, having an idiosyncratic style all their own.

April 1 - 10   Elm
The elm tree was associated with communication as its wood was used for making cart wheels. Elm is a tree associated with communication, and many born in this sign share a love of language.

They are voracious readers, erudite and eloquent, with the ability to express themselves in both a vivid and witty manner. Elm people are natural communicators and others may find themselves captivated by their tales and anecdotes. Many are excellent speakers with a natural ability to entertain and encourage others. Sometimes, however, their sense of humour can be sarcastic or cutting and others may take offence.

11 - 20 April   Larch

Those born in the Larch sign share an active intellect, together with a strong sense of intuition. Self-reliance and determination play an important part in ensuring the Larch success.

The Larch has a highly energetic personality, coupled with keen powers of observation. Most are charitable and altruistic, although sometimes eccentric in their ways. They are fast on the uptake, quick to seize the initiative and are always eager for new experiences. Many are good at sports and physical activities and can sometimes be obsessive in their pursuits.

21 - 30 April   Box

Those born during the Box sign are noted for their adaptability and versatility. However, they tend to lack a singleness of purpose and powers of concentration need deliberate cultivation.

Otherwise, even though they have more creative potential than people born in many other signs, they may not make the most of their talents. Box people generally spread themselves in too many different directions at one time.

On the positive side, those born in this sign tend to have a remarkable ability to handle many things at one time.

1 - 12 May   Rowan

Having natural charm, those born in the Rowan cycle are both expressive and theatrical. With easily stimulated emotions, they have tremendous enthusiasm for new ideas. They share an originality of thinking with a quick intellect and good memory. The Rowan has the capacity to learn easily. They have a romantic temperament coupled with great love of travel and adventure.

Neat and tidy, the Rowan person takes pride in their personal appearance. This is an extremely artistic and creative sign, although those born in it may suffer from an overactive imagination.

13 -25 May   Cherry

Blessed with an abundance of mental energy, Cherry people are capable of handling most tasks that befall them.

Those born in this sign possess intellectual vitality, mental dexterity and a lively imagination. The Cherry is one of the most eloquent of signs and many can argue an opponent blue in the face. Those born in this cycle have endless optimism for their chosen pursuits. They have a deep sense of intuition and seem to know precisely what others are thinking and planning.

26 May - 7 June   Hawthorn

Those born in the Hawthorn sign have a determined
spirit with much capacity for creative thinking. They share
a sympathetic and hospitable personality and spiritual
aspirations are usually well developed. The Hawthorn
has a generous nature and an idealistic attitude to life.

The common good is usually a high priority for the Hawthorn
who is prepared to make many a personal sacrifice to help
those around them. Sadly, however, the generosity of those
born in this sign can mean that they are often exploited by
others.

8 - 20 June   Oak

Those born in this cycle are strong and resolute, others
looking to them for guidance.

The Oak person, however, can often fail to understand those
less strong, finding it incomprehensible that the tasks they
find easy others may find hard. They make excellent leaders,
so long as they remember not to overtax their followers. If
left without a challenge, the Oak may lapse into a state of
lethargy, content to watch the world go by.

21 - 30 June   Aspen

Particularly conscientious concerning most endeavours,
those born in the Aspen sign often play leading roles in
political organizations or social groups.

Few born in this sign are inclined to do anything on the spur of the moment and most are averse to change. The Aspen person has firm opinions and convictions. Anything to which the Aspen's mind is set is well within the realms of possibility. They have a practical attitude to life and are seldom ones for dreaming, reminiscing or fantasizing. The Aspen person can however be too materialistic and cynical.

1 - 10 July   Spindle
Those born in the Spindle sign have exceptional powers of leadership and strong willpower is matched by excellent executive skills.

With considerable ability for making money, the Spindle person is always willing to devote time and effort towards the success of an enterprise. Strongly principled, they often possess great courage and are reliable and trustworthy. They can, however, be overbearing and arrogant.

11 - 21 July   Linden
Lindens are often over-cautious and share a stubborn reluctance to take chances. They may be highly competent organizers and administrators, but experimentation and risk taking is best left to others.

Sometimes their hesitance can be a handicap: frequently they fail to exploit their capabilities or realize their full potential. For the best results, the Linden should learn to take the occasional risk and realize that failures are often an important part of learning. Although those born in the Linden sign are affectionate and loving, they have a tendency to become clingy or overbearing in relationships.

22 – 31 July   Poplar

Those born in the Poplar sign will take a central role in social activities. They are always ready to give advice and are often the best shoulder on which to cry.

Their own problems, however, they keep to themselves, being the last to worry others with their own concerns. It is so difficult to tell what the Poplar person is thinking or, more importantly, how they are feeling. People born in this sign tend to be emotional and sometimes far to sentimental for their own good.

1 - 13 August   Birch

Those born in the sign of the Birch share an unusual combination of both the materialistic and the imaginative.

One of the chief characteristics of the Birch personality is to constantly question the world about them. They are both analytical and self-critical, sometimes to the extent of impeding progress. However, the Birch person can achieve remarkable results in a very short time. In social circumstances the Birch is often the one to initiate, plan and organize events. Sometimes, however, they make try to organize others to much.

14 -26 August   Privet

Those born in the Privet sign are practical and realistic regarding relationships. They never expect too much and are prepared to work towards a long and happy marriage. If a relationship fails, however, they are well prepared to move on, providing they know that the situation is really hopeless. Seldom holding grudges, the Privet person is always ready to forgive. They do not tend to make good business people, however, as they are not hard and ruthless enough to succeed. They do, however, make excellent teachers, trainers and advisors.

27 August - 8 September   Chestnut

Those born in the Chestnut sign have great versatility. Endowed with an alert mind and an excellent memory, they are capable of solving many problems that others find difficult.

They are especially precise regarding minute detail. Neat and methodical, they take pride in their work. In business, they work best alone, being capable of long periods of devoted activity. Philosophical interests are a marked feature, with considerable originality of ideas. Those born in the Chestnut sign do, however, tend to become so wrapped up in their own work, hobbies or pursuits that they can become isolated from those around them.

9 – 20 September   Buckthorn

Although somewhat fussy or faddy, the person born in the Buckthorn sign is good in social circumstances.

At ease in the company of both sexes, they have an entertaining sense of humour and a versatile character, making them the soul of any party. However, the Buckthorn person often gives the impression that they are not quite sharing the spirit of the occasion as they are usually thinking of more than one thing at once.

21 - 30 September   Elder
The Elder was a symbol of knowledge and those born in this sign often exude an aura of wisdom. They have logical and calculating minds, formulating plans and waiting patiently for the precise moment to act.

Although they enjoy the virtue of patience, they live constantly in a state of readiness. They are eager to learn and quick to find practical applications for their knowledge. So often it is the Elder person who is called upon to deal with the problems others have failed to solve. Elder people make good and loyal friends but can hold grudges and so make bad enemies.

1 - 10 October   Maple
Those born in the Maple cycle exercise enviable patience concerning most endeavours and accurately judge the correct moment to act.

They also have the capacity to grasp the root of a problem, possessing shrewd insight into the real cause of difficulties they may face. In any enterprise the Maple will weigh up its potential long and hard before making decisions. Maple people can, however, be somewhat judgmental of friends and loved ones and have a tendency to hold a conservative outlook on life.

11 - 20 October   Beech

Those born in the Beech sign are forthright and astute; they have inquiring and probing minds and are remarkably self-disciplined.

However, they sometimes tend to disregard the ideas and feelings of others and act thoughtlessly. Nevertheless, they are honest and few will find the Beech person conniving or underhand. Those born in this sign make excellent problem solvers

21 – 30 October   Dogwood

Those born in the dogwood cycle have a serious outlook on life, coupled with a strong sense of responsibility.

Their ambition is supported by a shrewd intellect and the ability to devote themselves exclusively to an enterprise. Observant and inquisitive, the Dogwood person is quick to learn. They are especially loyal to their friends and take family values seriously. They may though tend to be to judgmental and have a tendency to be somewhat opinionated in their views

31 October - 12 November   Juniper

The main characteristic of those born in the sign of the Juniper is the ability to create possibilities from very little.

They are optimistic in the extreme, seldom accepting anything as hopeless. Usually able to find some good even in their worst enemies, the Juniper is remarkably resilient. They have a close affinity with nature and are often conservationists and vegetarians. Life is an adventure for the Juniper, although a craving for excitement may lead to tricky situations. Always eager for new experiences, and ready to rise to the challenge, the Juniper's life is full of surprise. They may, however, be a little naive in their attitude to life.

13 – 25 November   Broom

Resilient, optimistic and determined, those born in the Broom sign have an inventive and adaptable personality.

They are industrious and highly active, with the ability to find new uses for the most unlikely things. Technically gifted regarding the crafts, the Broom person has a conscientious attitude to work. There is a strong tendency to champion the plight of the unfortunate, and an enviable power to inspire confidence and enthusiasm in others. Unfortunately, however, those born in this sign find it difficult to make up their minds.

26 November - 8 December   Blackthorn

Although they see the best in most people, those born in the Blackthorn sign dislike arrogance and hate aggression. They are kind and sympathetic to those who are shy or in distress; it is often the Blackthorn person who comes to the aid of those in trouble. They are never boring to be around but their need for solitude can sometimes be taken the wrong way and friends might feel they have done something to offend.

9 - 20 December   Yew

Those born in the Yew sign have a stubborn streak. They prefer to do things their own way - even when they know they are wrong. Often a dreamer, the Yew person may refuse to face reality when problems occur.

They are deep thinkers and extremely creative. This is a sign of the musicians, artists and writers.

Tree of (dwindling) Knowledge

A recent survey reported that one in twenty of the people interviewed couldn't identify any of the common native trees they were shown. 31% recognised the horse chestnut but fewer realised they produced conkers and only 5% could identify hazel.

It was the older people surveyed who knew the most but also admitted not passing their knowledge down to younger generations.

There are numerous little 'Tree Finder' guides available that will fit easily into a pocket and plenty of beautiful parks and woodlands on our doorstep. So please, make a commitment to get out in the fresh air and 'teach your child, or yourself, a tree.'

The Gift(s) of Gardening

I love giving gifts with a personal touch and one of the nicest ways to do that is to give a plant with a special meaning.

Roses are probably the easiest plant to find a suitably named variety with names including, 'I love You', 'Congratulations', 'Lovely Lady', 'Blessings', 'Thank you', 'My Mum/Dad/Love', 'Birthday Wishes', 'Devotion', 'Just Married', 'Friend for Life', 'Good Luck', 'Superstar', 'Loving Memory' amongst many others.

If you are looking for an alternative Easter present to give rather than a chocolate egg, why not give packets of seeds or a plant. Chocolate cosmos is a topical choice of plant and the beautiful velvety, deep crimson blooms do really smell of chocolate. Or maybe an Egg plant, (aubergine) for the kitchen garden or even the 'poached egg' plant that is fabulous for attracting hoverflies, bees and butterflies into the garden; sow the seeds over Easter weekend and you'll have eye catching flowers that look just like poached eggs, in the summer.

Then there is the Stachys lanata, commonly known as 'lambs ears' or 'rabbits ears' as the leaves are soft and furry just like the animals ears.

A word of warning though, unless the recipient is a very keen gardener, or on a diet, it may be a good idea to put a *small* box of chocolates or Easter egg with the plant!

Weed 'em and Reap

No doubt you will have noticed the incredible bright yellow carpets of dandelions that are becoming more abundant every year. Still largely considered to be a weed, young dandelion leaves can be eaten in a salad or sandwich and are also known as wild endive. The leaves contain numerous vitamins, including more vitamin A than carrots. However, in France the name for dandelion is "pis-en-lit" meaning wet-your-bed, so the French tend to discourage young children from eating dandelion salads with their evening meal! In homeopathy, dandelion essence is used to treat overexertion and the feeling of doing too much and I am a firm believe that an abundance of a specific plant will indicate an ailment or condition that needs healing. Anyone feeling they're doing too much lately?

Chickweed is a highly versatile 'culinary weed'. It makes a great summer soup and is highly nutritious when juiced as well as adding a delicate flavour to salads. It can also be used in sandwiches instead of watercress, or lettuce. Wash the leaves well before using.

Scurvy-grass is a genus of 30 species of annual and perennial herbs in the cabbage family. Also known as Spoonwort because of the spoon shaped leaves the plant is rich in Vitamin C and was therefore eaten by sailors suffering from scurvy after long voyages. The leaves have a strong peppery taste similar to the related watercress and horseradish and can also be used in salads.

Celebrity Chit-Chat with Howard Marks

Described as 'the most sophisticated drugs baron of all time', Howard Marks admitted he has never actually grown any plants. "Well, I tried to grow marijuana once in the 70's, during the Miner's Strike," he added. "Some friends came across some chemicals that were supposed to improve the growth. They made the plants into good rope but useless dope, so I've never bothered since."

"I've never had to grow my own," he chuckled, "People always ask me for tips on growing marijuana but the truth is I haven't a clue, although I am sincerely interested in the finished product. I've never grown it but I've smuggled loads and I belong to a company that produces seeds for sale wherever its legal to do so, called Mr Nice Seed Bank.

"A lot of people I speak to have got into growing marijuana through botany. They know a lot more about it than I do." The laid back Welshman continued, "I like the fresh air and spend quite a bit of time outdoors in the course of my travelling. I often visit gardens and parks and would much rather walk through a park or public garden than along the street. Apart from my obvious favourite plant, I have always liked rhododendrons; they are the first exciting flower I remember noticing. I like snowdrops too as they're the first you notice in the year, or they used to be until it all got f***ed up. I like daffodils too but I think that's just the link with Wales."

Howard is obviously very fond of Wales and is back there often. "My favourite place still has to be Kenfig Hill, where I was brought up, for nostalgic reasons but I think the further west you go the more interesting it gets. My second favourite place is Dinas Island which is why it features strongly in my crime fiction novel 'Sympathy for the Devil'."

Despite a lack of interest in gardening, Howard admitted to being fanatical about things he does enjoy. "It only usually lasts about a week but that's usually long enough to learn something new. I learned how to play Bowls, attracted by the fact that it was made illegal in the 16th Century. There were only two sports then, archery and bowls. Archery was OK as it encouraged the British to fire arrows into the French but as there was no destructive element in Bowls, it was made illegal in England for 400 years.

"I tried golf when I came out of prison in 1982 but didn't enjoy it. Swinging a club is an unnatural movement and the social side is a bit dubious too. Though I enjoyed getting p***ed afterwards."

"I don't like zoos either," he added randomly, adding with a chuckle, "it's all to do with being caged up. I'm not keen."

As well as several autobiographies, Howard has written a series of crime thrillers.
www.howardmarks.name

Get Stoned

Rocks are revered as the 'bones' of a Japanese garden and it is recommended to include a tall vertical stone, a low vertical stone and a horizontal stone.

Stones are best placed as a group of three but can be in two's to represent male and female. There are also stones to avoid – the 'diseased stone', (one with a misshapen or disfigured top); the 'dead stone', (a stone with a horizontal grain that is propped upright, like a dead body) and the 'pauper stone', (a stone that bears no relation to any other stone in the garden).

In any garden, rockeries should be constructed with natural stone set well into the soil to resemble a natural outcrop. Avoid the 'current bun' – a rockery with stones placed on the soil surface and the 'dog's grave' - using a single, isolated stone.

The Japanese also consider it to be important to be able to visit a garden in all seasons, and winter is as important as any other season. Architectural planting, such as Acers and bonsai trees, boast a beautiful framework of branches in the absence of leaves and a dusting of snow on trees is called 'sekku', or 'snow blossom'.

The wonderful philosophy associated with Japanese gardening is that one shouldn't create anything that nature wouldn't, so no square ponds or fountains.

The apparent emptiness - a sharp contrast to our busy and full Western gardens - helps create a feeling of space, promoting peace and stillness. Boulders are used to represent mountains, and raked gravel donates the continual flow of water. It is also important for the space to be enclosed as the garden is perceived as being a separate world that one can visit leaving behind their worries and concerns.

Open Minds and Being Kind

One of my favourite authors, Lyall Watson has written many thought-provoking and visionary books including the best-seller Supernature, Gifts of Unknown Things and The Jacobson's Organ. Many years ago, another of his books, The Secret Life of Inanimate Objects resonated with me, leading me to explore his perspective on the secret life of inanimate objects.

As Desmond Morris, author of The Naked Ape says, "there is nothing worse than a close mind. Lyall Watson's strength lies in his readiness to find and study strange phenomena without the fears other scientists have."

As well as suggesting we are able to form a bond with valued objects, which explains their 'uncanny' reappearance if lost, (Geoff Slater, of Haverford West in Wales found a gold ring in his garden and with the help of the hallmark was able to return it to Viv Stoddard who lived 20 miles away. The day of the 'surprise reunion' was also her 20th wedding anniversary), Lyall shares incidents where computers have been 'fixed' by simply being nice to them. Our reactions have unfortunately evolved to shout at and berate something which isn't working for us, which is obviously channelling negative energy toward the object and focussing on the fact that it isn't working, all of which is counter-productive. Try adopting a pleasant approach and you may be pleasantly surprised.

One of my favourite examples of communicating with an inanimate object was to explain nicely to an old mower, which stubbornly refused to fire and start after 20 minutes of exhaustive effort, that although it was actually it's prerogative to chose not to cut the grass, if it continued to favour that option then another mower would be brought in as a replacement and it would be scrapped. Harsh but appropriate.

After the little pep talk, the mower burst into life on the second pull of the cord.

Lyall also gives examples of various communications with to rocks. He suggests that as silicon is a kind of crystal which lies at the heart of our whole electronics industry - making transistors, semi conductors and microchips possible - that all stone, which after all is largely crystalline, should be seen as a sort of macro chip; a natural, if somewhat haphazard, electronic system capable of storing energies and given the right circumstances, playing them back at a later date.

She Rocks!

A dear friend, Ariana Houle, has written a book about her own journey conversing with rocks, called "Conversations with Nature" and suggests that we have been communicating with rocks for years just 'on another level'. She asks, "What made you pick up that little rock and take it home?" She also points out just how many people have a 'special' rock or stone that they have picked up and kept, having a connection with it, be it a conscious one or not. Like Lyall, Ariana's strength lies in exploring an unconventional path. It makes compelling reading.

You can contact her at *naturespeakspublishing@yahoo.com*

Super Seeds and Sprouts

If you want to grow your own green stuff through the winter, the windowsill is an ideal spot. Sprouting seeds are incredibly easy to grow and are tasty and nutritious. They are great to add to soups and stews as well as sandwiches and salads and a Sprouting Kit also makes a fabulous present for keen gardeners and potential gardeners of all ages.

Chose from an interesting range of seeds to sprout, including sunflower seeds, broccoli, radish, mustard and even clover, for £1.95 per packet.

You can buy a Sprouter Unit, (around £15.00), seeds and good books on the subject online or from most good garden centres.

Native American Wisdom

I have heard it said that every time two people meet, one of them is learning, one is teaching. I have much gratitude to singer/songwriter Michael Dimitri and his wife Athena for all that they taught me during our meetings. Apart from telling some great stories as a result of working with many amazing music legends, their Native American roots have provided them with incredible insights into the spiritual guidance that Nature offers.

Mike shared, "I embrace the Native American ways. They share a love and respect for family and Nature and honour Grandmother Earth (Nokimis Akiin). We always pray to the seeds before sowing and again to the plants before harvesting, it's about respecting what the Earth is providing for us.

"Native American tradition recognises four sacred plants as gifts for the Four Manido (Spirits of the Four Directions). The Creator taught us to use sage, sweet grass, tobacco and cedar to remind us of Great Spirits and the importance of giving thanks and gratitude for what we have. When the elders smoke tobacco in their sacred pipes the smoke isn't inhaled, it is used to take away evil spirits and negativity. It is believed to connect the worlds as the roots of tobacco go deep into the soil and the smoke goes high into the sky, linking the two. Tobacco is also used as an offering. Whenever we take something from Nature or the earth, we explain to the plants or tree why we are doing it and then offer a little bit of tobacco as a token of gratitude and respect.

"Of course Native tobacco is different to what you smoke in the UK. Sacred tobacco, Nicotiana rustica, doesn't contain any nicotine or toxins, unlike your tobacco which we call Nicotiana Bigbucks," he laughed.

"Cedar is also burnt to cleanse negativity, to bless a house and whilst meditating. You can put a little cedar in your shoe for good things to come to you and many women on the Reservations carry cedar in their left pocket. Breathing in cedar will fill you with courage.

"Sage dissolves negativity and cleanses as well as offering protection. Carrying a bit of sage with you or in your car will help keep you safe. Spirits love the fragrant smoke and it attracts their attention which makes prayer more powerful.

"Sweet grass is usually braided to represent the united tribe and the smoke stimulates the mind, cleanses the body and also welcomes spirit. It's all about giving gratitude and honouring the earth, like the proverb says;

Treat the Earth well. It was not given to you by your parents, it was loaned to you by your children. We do not inherit the Earth from our Ancestors. We borrow it from our children."

Madeiran Cold Remedy

Put 5 crushed garlic cloves in frying pan with 5 tablespoons sugar and very slowly dissolve the sugar. Add 2 cups milk and heat to simmer. Blend and reheat. Drink whilst hot.

See the cough off

A traditional recipe to get rid of a stubborn cough and cold.

- 1 medium purple onion
- 1 kg bag of brown sugar
- A med stainless steel bowl
- A glass jar.

Directions:

- Cut the onion into thin ring slices.
- Layer the bottom of the bowl with sugar.
- Place a thin layer of onion rings over the sugar.
- Place another layer of sugar over the onion.
- Continue layering until all onion and sugar is used.
- Try to end up with sugar on top.
- Cover the stainless steel bowl with a cling wrap.
- Place in the sunny spot of the home and leave to stand a minimum of 24 hours. 30 is best!
- Pour off the liquid that has risen to the top of the bowl into the glass container.
- Stop pouring when you see sugar.
- Seal and keep in fridge for no more then one month.

Take a tablespoon-full twice a day for a cold or a teaspoon full when coughing.

I am not anti-social,
I am just pro-solitude

Wise old Sage

Sage falls into two camps, the genus Salvia which relates to the mint family and is dominant across Europe and the genus Armetisia belonging to the daisy or aster family. The sages preferred by the Native Americans are armetisias though salvias are also used.

Salvia comes from the Latin 'to cure'. As well as it's healing and spiritual qualities, sage is a great addition to the garden visually and evergreen qualities. Choose salvia officinalis 'Kew Gold' for yellow leaves, 'purpurascens' for reddish-purple leaves and the striking 'tricolour' for its pretty mottles foliage.

Leaf Grief

A man who had fallen in love with a tree killed himself when building workers cut it down during road works. Eighty-three-year-old Milan Fabac shot himself in front of the road builders in Zlatar, northern Croatia, after telling neighbours he couldn't go on without the oak.

Pest of British

The RHS listed last year's Top Five Garden Pests as:
1. Slugs and snails
2. Cushion scale
3. Vineweevil
4. Ants
5. Viburnum beetle

Good Rid-Ants!

A recent survey shows that ants are the fourth most disliked garden pests after wasps, spiders and slugs. Ants are naturally repelled by quite a few spices, herbs and powders so have a look what you have in your store cupboard and sprinkle a little of your chosen 'weapon' wherever the ants are coming in.

Choose from powdered charcoal, turmeric, cinnamon, citrus oil, cayenne pepper, chalk lines, Vaseline (great for doors and windows), white vinegar, crushed mint leaves, lavender oil and oil of clove or crushed cloves. Bay leaves are also effective for keeping ants away from specific foods.
They are especially attracted to sugar and flour, so putting bay leaves in your storage jars will help.

Ants are also extremely susceptible to caffeine which they can't digest.

If you leave coffee grounds (used work as well as fresh) where the ants can reach them they will carry them home to eat. It is a bit grim though, as it causes a lingering death which also means the results will take a few weeks to notice.

If you fancy your ants chocolate coated, then pop into the 'insect candy store', at *www.hotlix.com*; as well as chocol-ants, they also offer chocolate covered worms, salt and vinegar crickets and cheese and onion flavoured crickets. Be warned though, actor and presenter Stephen Fry admitted finding the chocolate covered insects, repell'ant'!

I Spied the Spider

Many people claim that bringing conkers, the fruit of the horse chestnut, indoors and placing on windowsills and in corners of the room will keep spiders out of the house. And I have found it does work to a degree, with more research suggesting that it is because the brown skin of the conker contains triterpenoid saponin, which is a natural insect repellent.

If you want to try the theory out, why not get creative too and make conker swags or experiment with other ornamental options.

A cobweb is a spider's web that has been abandoned. Most spiders use their web to entangle and capture their prey, but not all spiders need to create webs to catch food. The Wolf spider stalks and overtakes his prey whilst the Jumping spider simply pounces on his!

Also making the list of biggest house pests are those long-legged spiders that look a little like crane flies. They are in fact the Pholcidae family of spiders and the confusion arises as they are, like crane flies, also known as Daddy-Long-Legs. They weave irregular messy webs, unlike the intricate creations synonymous with most spiders, and although they prefer cellars (they are also known as Cellar-spiders) and attics they will also inhabit dark, quiet corners of the house too. If disturbed, they vibrate (hence yet another name, 'Vibrating spiders') to confuse their attacker, a method they also use to attract their prey.

Apparently they are quite useful at keeping the house clear of other spiders and insects and alarmingly, when food is short they tend to eat their next of kin!

Their biggest predator is the vacuum cleaner, which reminds me: *"God gave us rain so gardener's can do their housework."*

Not Mushroom in Here ...

The fact that mushrooms seem to 'appear overnight' is because they are capable of pulling up an incredible amount of moisture from the soil very quickly, enabling them to expand rapidly. They can swell from a pinhead to being obvious in just a few hours following heavy rain, hence the term 'mushrooming' for something that grows quickly.

A Fun Guy

Although keen on foraging in general I've never been much of a fan of foraging for fungi or mushrooms as I've never really trusted them.

It seems I am not alone but forager and author of Fungi Forays, Daniel Butler is keen to encourage us all to be braver when it comes to picking and eating wild mushrooms. He explained, "Last year five people were killed in bucket related accidents and 91 people died falling out of bed. No one died from eating a poisonous mushroom."

It is this refreshing and reassuring approach that will endear you to the fungi forager. "Beginners are often intimidated by too many varieties so it is better to slowly build up a repertoire of what you know and what you like. They all taste different and you probably won't like most of them. The Puffballs are foolproof, you can't get them wrong but I don't think they are worth the taste.

"The best beginner's mushroom meets three criteria. Firstly, choose something that is very distinctive in appearance like Chicken of the Woods (the yellow dinner-plate fungi which grows on Oak trees).

"Secondly, make sure there are no possible dangerous look-a-likes and thirdly, if you do finally pluck up courage to eat what you have harvested, make sure you get the maximum taste reward. The Porcini or cep is a good one to start with.

These are one of the few mushrooms that taste better dried than fresh so are good to pick and store."

I explained to Daniel that my father, Bob, used to absolutely love field and horse mushrooms, so much so that I remember many unprecedented stops in lay-bys if mushrooms were spotted in an adjacent field. Unfortunately wild mushrooms didn't like him and after enjoying them in a much anticipated fry up, he would be stopping at lay-bys a little later for a different reason altogether.

Daniel was keen to explain why. "Most field mushrooms are edible and closely related to the mushrooms you buy in the shops however there is one called a Yellow Stainer, which bruises yellow. It's edible for 50% of people but 50% will have an allergic reaction and will spend a couple of hours on the toilet. Mushrooms are also intense in protein and often quite hard to digest for many people. But it's worth persevering. Generally poisonous ones taste disgusting and you'll throw up before you ingest enough of it to kill you," he added cheerfully.

Daniel has recently collated a series of essays as a Kindle book, 'A Mushroom is a Misunderstood Rose'. Dispelling many fears and myths it is also packed with fascinating fungi facts, as Daniel shared, "A lot of mushrooms have a symbiotic relationship with trees. 99% of plants couldn't survive without fungi and neither could humans. We are very ignorant about them and their virtues. On a cellular level, mushrooms are closer to humans than plants."

I asked him about the Fairy Ring on my own lawn.

"The Fairy Ring Champignon is a gorgeous tasting mushroom," he started off encouragingly, "but it does have a poisonous look alike. Once you know that, they are very easy to tell apart. Just have a look in Fungi Forays!"

Find out more and sign up for his fabulous newsletter at *www.fungiforays.co.uk*

Honey (fungus) I'm home

If you have ever had the misfortune to encounter the dreaded honey fungus in your garden then take heart, the World's largest living thing is actually a honey fungus in Oregon, USA which covers a whopping 10,000 acres.

Novelty Plants

I always grow a few novelty plants each year and each year the list gets longer.

I'm especially keen to try the New Zealand Yam (exclusive to Thompson & Morgan). These unusual tubers have a nutty lemony flavour, and are available in spring, to be harvested in November and December. You can also use the shamrock-like leaves in salads. I also love the Kale Walking Sticks or Jersey cabbage. The 6ft stem makes a great walking stick and the leaves can be harvested as any other Kale.

Other lofty plants I have marvelled at include the Mongolian Giant sunflower which can reach up to 15 ft., a huge hibiscus, called Giant Hardy producing flowers that reach a staggering 1ft across from mid-summer to autumn; giant fuchsias boasting blooms of 4 inches across, (4 times the size of a normal flower head) and giant geraniums that are also weather resistant.

My favourites though are the tremendous Tree Lilies that will grow to 8ft tall in just two years. Just give these sweet smelling stunners some support and they will come back year after year with one bulb producing over 30 trumpet blooms. Or choose the Crystal Tree Lilies that grow over 6 ft in the first year, are double flowering and bloom for twice as long as the standard Tree Lilies. They make a fabulous scented hedgerow.

I also like the sound of Lofos, with their cascades of blooms and the new Vulcan Grass with its fan shaped seed heads which will be great for indoor displays as well as feeding the birds. The sweet pepper, Sweet Sunshine has a unique trailing habit making it ideal for growing in hanging baskets and is described as 'vigorous and ornamental' as well as productive. Each plant produces 200-300 little fruits that can be picked from the end of July to the first frosts. For novelty value try Heartbreaker tomato seeds, which will provide beautiful little heart shaped cherry tomatoes and Purple Majesty seed potatoes which are supposed to be great for chips with the purple flesh making purple fries.

And I keep meaning to introduce the intriguingly named Flower of Death, (Lisianthius nigrescens) to the cottage garden. It is a rare exotic plant, little known outside its native homeland of Mexico, with tubular flowers of the darkest black, on slender, towering stems. It will make a dramatic specimen plant and a fascinating talking point that will create interest and wonder at the back of borders. But it is a half-hardy perennial so will require winter protection in a frost free environment during the winter months.

I am always tempted by 'easy-to-grow' varieties which are more tolerant of metrological mood swings. Like the new variety of runner bean called Moonlight that is guaranteed to set beans in any weather and a 'weatherproof' outdoor basil, which is more tolerant of cold, wet and windy weather (Basil British Basil). Another favourite is the fabulous Common Milkweed (Asclepias syriaca) from www.bakkers.co.uk with fruits which look just like little parrots.

They're always great to tweet or squawk about!
And, of course, packets of seeds make great presents and
are easy to post inside a card.

Embrace your shadows;
Where there are shadows
there is light.

Young Luffas

If you fancy growing your own dishcloth, plant the seed of
the Luffa vine about the middle of May. In the autumn the
gourds produced on this vine will be ready to harvest.

Cut open lengthwise and take out the fibrous mass inside,
thoroughly wash in hot soapy water to remove pulp and
seeds, then dry in the sun and you will have your dishcloth
ready for use.

For more info and a step by step guide visit *www.luffa.info.*

Personali-trees

Whether you are a gardener or not, you will almost certainly
have a favourite plant, tree or shrub. During thirty years of
gardening, I have noticed that people's choices of preferred
plants actually reflects aspects of their own personalities.
So I wrote a book about it. 'Personali-trees' offers a tongue-
in-cheek insight to someone's personality based on their
choice of preferred plant. And here are a few examples:

SWEET PEA (LATHYRUS)
You are a keen gardener and probably grow your own
your vegetables and herbs. You have a lot of inherited
antiques in your home and haven't bought much of your
own furniture. You detest salesmen and being put on hold
on the telephone. You enjoy good wines and good food but
have a tendency to over-indulge. Gout could be a problem
for you in later life.

Petals of wisdom: Never play leapfrog with a unicorn.

JAPANESE MAPLE (ACER)
You are pretentious and outspoken but consider them to
be positive qualities. You possess a confident charm and
people like you. You don't suffer fools at all, let alone gladly
but don't bear grudges either. Physically you are likely to
be lithe and fit with enormous amounts of stamina. You
always eat breakfast and could well be a vegetarian.

Petals of wisdom: Forgive your enemies but never forget
their names.

LILY (LILIUM)
You are a strong character, determined but fair and with
a core of steel. You have chiselled features and are very

good-looking although a little bemused by attention from the opposite sex. You are seldom without several admirers though people don't really ever 'know' you. You are capable of great things but often lead a very unassuming lifestyle. Solitude is very important to you and you tend to retreat often to rescue and restore your inner peace.

Petals of wisdom: Beauty is only skin deep but ugly goes
right to the bone.

SAGE (SALVIA)
Oh Wise One, you are unassuming but 'deep' and mystical. You believe in truth and integrity and cannot abide liars, cheats or deceit. Conventional and diplomatic are not words that are in your vocabulary and you will have spent time in a retreat. You are hopeless with money and drink too much coffee.

Petals of wisdom: Father doesn't hear what Mother says but
Mother hears what Father doesn't say.

SNOWDROP (GALANTHUS)
You are extremely popular amongst your friends, family and work colleagues. You are always upbeat, see the best in people and are always willing to help out. You enjoy making things happen and although a little apprehensive about change, largely you thrive on a challenge and are undeterred by paperwork or legislation. You are not a 'morning' person and dislike getting wet and cold.

Petals of wisdom: Sometimes when we don't get what we
want, it's a blessing.

HORSE CHESTNUT (AESCULES)

You are reliable and resourceful though still very much a child at heart. You don't relish responsibilities and would like to take time out of the office to go and play "pooh-sticks" again. Cheerful and optimistic, you would rather learn by your own mistakes than listen to the advice of others. You love skiing, hot tubs and winter holidays in general.

Petals of wisdom: Life is too short to wait.

FLOWERING CHERRY/PLUM/ALMOND (PRUNUS)

Oooooh! You are such a 'girlie' at heart. You love being spoilt and love lots and lots of attention. You dream of being swept off your feet by a knight in shining armour (yep, even if you are a fella!) and will throw your toys out of your pram if things don't go your way. You are the original Drama Queen and people love you for it!

Petals of wisdom: Dance as though no one's watching, sing as though no one is listening and love as though you've never been hurt.

HONEYSUCKLE (LONICERA)

You are a bit of a 'wannabe' nomad and love the thought of travelling around Europe in a camper van. However you are also in a well paid and fairly secure job and prefer a regular pay-check at the moment. If you do travel, it will be later in life. You move slowly, are clumsy and would rather lie on a couch than sit on it. You always have control of the TV remote and like crisps in sandwiches.

Petals of wisdom: Never judge anyone until you have walked a mile in their shoes, than at least you'll have a new pair of shoes.

JASMINE (JASMINIUM)

You are an idealist with very high expectations. You love socialising but inevitably find fault with the venue, service or company. People find you hard work as you always appear to be dissatisfied. You are pedantic. You never carry cash and have several credit cards. Managing money is not your strong point and you like trading skills instead of paying for things.

Petals of wisdom: Outside of a dog, a book is a man's best friend. Inside a dog, it's too dark to read.

LAVENDER (LAVANDULA)

You are an old fashioned romantic who believes the hero always gets his girl. You love TV soaps, good films and most other forms of escapism. You wear lots of practical, sensible clothes and shoes and enjoy browsing the Charity shops. You are excellent at remembering people's birthdays and other important dates. You were close to your Grandmother and probably had a pet rabbit as a child.

Petals of wisdom: Happiness is simply good health and a poor memory.

OAK (QUERCUS)

You have an abundance of common sense and think laterally. Honesty is paramount to you and you are an excellent listener. You are probably in a long-term relationship and are extremely loyal and faithful to your partner. You are very strong physically and take good care of your health. You will get to the top of your chosen vocation at a young age and dislike wearing a suit.

Petals of wisdom: Make small decisions with the head and big ones from the heart.

ROSE (ROSA)

Climbing/rambling: you are clingy and co-dependant, with a tendency for emotional and dramatic outbursts. You are also intelligent enough to know that dramatic outbursts are not productive and are embarrassed afterwards.

Hybrid T: you are a traditionalist and dislike progress. You are an incurable romantic and are constantly in pursuit of a loving relationship. You have big hips and are good company to be with.

Shrub: you are very secure and self confident without being arrogant. You have a fabulous aura and an enviable inner calm. People love to be around you.

Petals of wisdom: People can be divided into 3 groups: those who make things happen; those who watch things happen and those who wonder what's happening.

STRAW FLOWER (HELICHRYSUM)

You lack self-confidence and self-esteem. You are very nostalgic with the past playing a big part in your life. You often harp back to the way things used to be. This is largely because you are afraid of the future. Being indecisive, you are terrified of making a wrong decision and are constantly worried what people think about you. You probably own a cat as a dog would be too demanding.

Petals of wisdom: Don't cry because it's the end; smile because it's the beginning.

IF YOU PREFER EVERGREENS, CONIFERS AND GROUND COVER PLANTS then you like value for money and dislike extravagance – unless someone else is paying for you to be extravagant. You are quite cynical and sarcastic and have a clever, sharp wit.   Although you enjoy your privacy, you secretly yearn to be a 'head-liner' in a National newspaper and have the paparazzi camp on your doorstep. You enjoy strong cheese and red wine. Your kitchen will have a scrubbed wooden table as a centre piece and you can't be bothered to recycle anything. You will have kept many of your books from childhood and enjoy the Antiques Roadshow. Call centres infuriate you as does queuing. You also despise anything American and avoid fast food outlets. You were close to your Grandmother and still love the smell of home-baking.

Petals of wisdom: The only difference between a rut and a
grave is a few feet.

IF YOU PREFER BEDDING PLANTS AND ANNUALS then you worry a great deal about what other people think about you and dread upsetting someone, or anyone. Ironically, people love your company and you are a good host - you may even have made a career out of it. You probably belong to a 'group', committee or Neighbourhood Watch and a book club. You would rather drink from a cup and saucer than a mug and think fruit teas are pointless. You own at least one hat, scarf and glove set and always wear perfume or aftershave. You think traffic calming is a good idea and dislike 4x4 vehicles. You are loyal to the smaller, local shops. Your living room will be slightly impractical, probably with a light coloured carpet and a cream leather sofa and probably kept for best. You use an artificial tree for Christmas and buy Charity cards.

Petals of wisdom: Hurt me once, shame on you.
                             Hurt me twice, shame on me.

IF YOU PREFER ARCHITECTURAL PLANTS AND GRASSES then you are artistic, creative and have the potential to be rather flamboyant. You are often considered to be showing off but it is just your way. You love life. You probably live in a large house and are obsessively neat and tidy.   Australia holds a special place in your heart and you own a cuddly koala bear. You enjoyed school, always cleaned the blackboard and tended to be a bit of a teacher's pet. You would rather not have to work for a living and regularly do the lottery. You enjoy alcohol and probably smoking and socialise a lot. You have a shocking jealous streak, which you normally manage to hide well. You will always be comfortable financially either by your own endeavors or those of your partner.

Petals of wisdom: If you are clever, you will have the last
                             word. If you are really clever, you won't
                             use it.

A PREFERENCE FOR FRUIT AND VEGETABLES indicates that you are practical and hardworking and used to being the provider. You will probably have, or have had, a manual job though maybe retired now. You enjoy DIY and pottering and listening to the radio. You have big hands and have always got a bit of string in your pocket. Tea is your favourite drink (preferably with a piece of cake) and you seldom drink coffee. Your shed will be your sanctuary and you have lots of jars with different sized screws in them. You will have owned a van at some stage of your life and have probably 'caught' your own tea at least once. You think the world is 'going mad', despair with the Government and always have a nap on a Sunday afternoon.

Petals of wisdom: I am going to stand outside – if anyone asks, I'm outstanding.

IF YOU PREFER HERBS AND AROMATIC PLANTS then people see you as successful and centered but underneath a calm exterior you often feel in complete disarray. You have very high standards of everything and everyone, especially yourself and are your own biggest critic. A born achiever, you will probably never realise the extent of your accolades and will always be striving to be recognised and accepted. You are often in emotional turmoil as a result of being over analytical and will have dark times, which can be difficult for you. When you can keep it all together, you are fabulous company and people love you to bits. You often laugh until you cry and have a childlike wonderment of life. You don't understand why things should match and often wear odd socks. You are very energetic, sensual and passionate, performing best in the bedroom and the kitchen.

Petals of wisdom: If you must have an ego trip, best to travel light.

IF YOU LOVE WILDFLOWERS then you will love the outdoors and value nature hugely. You are very creative and will probably be a writer, musician and/or artist – or at least want to be. Although you are very gentle and rather spiritual, you also have an extremely stubborn streak and are a strong supporter of the causes you believe in. You are a real animal lover and will struggle with the inhumanity and injustices in life. However, you are also a 'doer' and very proactive so will inevitably do whatever you can to address the things that irritate and frustrate you. People think you are quite serious but you have a quirky sense of humour that is often overlooked by others, unless they share it! Your clothes are practical and comfortable and you hate dressing formally. You believe the truth is always the best policy, whether people want to hear it or not.

Petals of wisdom: When nothing goes right, go left.

The completely revised edition of Personali-trees is available from Amazon and *www.lynneallbutt.com*.

Bare-rooted ...

The Annual World Naked Gardening Day (WNGD) takes place annually on 5th May, when people across the globe are encouraged to tend their portion of the world's garden clothed as nature intended.

"The body seems to feel beauty when exposed to it as it feels the campfire or sunshine, entering not by the eyes alone, but equally through all one's flesh like radiant heat, making a passionate ecstatic pleasure glow not explainable."

- John Muir, founder of The Sierra Club

Find out more at www.wngd.org

A lovely quote from Tim Smit, famous for his work with the Eden Project and Lost Gardens of Heligan, (both in Cornwall);

"Since leaving the City and being involved in outdoor projects, I have become aware of just how important the weather is, especially to the people who work outdoors; it's not just something tacked onto the end of the News."

Celebrity Chit-Chat with Peter Gabriel

World renowned musician Peter Gabriel is also Head of Real World Records, the Founder of WOMAD, a Human Rights Activist and MIDEM's Personality of the Year ... and a keen gardener. "I was introduced to gardening when I was about 6 years old," he recalled, "my sister Anne and I each had a small patch to plant up in our parent's garden, between the swing and the house!

"I can't remember what we planted, probably annuals I think, but I enjoyed it then and I still do, though obviously I had more time at that young age. I love the wild English style gardening – the natural look. I love weaving willow too, it's therapeutic and it looks so good.

"I love to share my garden. The garden is a part of the whole living space. I don't like to distinguish between house and garden. I am very much a people person and have always been interested in what people do. I have a real sense of wonder at what they are doing and get enthusiastic for them!"

Has gardening ever influenced his music? "Of course," he laughed. "When I was with Genesis we did a track called Return of the Giant Hogweed and how it was taking over the World! The video for "Eve" featured beautiful scenes from Stourhead and "Don't Give Up" was written as a result of an American crop failure – it's about the drought and the plight of the farmers. Nature has a huge influence on everything, music included.

"That's why we should have more respect for it and the environment. There are a lot of good things happening but we need to keep on. By speeding up the development of SCiB, battery technology will soon be good enough for the development of electric cars and planes. That would really make a difference."

In 1999, Peter also instigated the formation of a new group of World Leaders known as the Elders . "Richard (Branson) and I thought there should be a new gathering of 'Elders', like traditional village elders, that would come together to guide and support our 'global village'. The result is powerful group of people who have nothing to prove and who can speak freely and boldly. Their only agenda is for humanity. They believe that despite the awful things that are happening globally, all human beings are made for goodness.

"I wrote the music for the Pixar movie called WALL -E, which is about a robot and waste alleviation – it's very funny and will also raise awareness of the rubbish we generate. We can't afford to relax about getting these messages across."

Talking of relaxing, how does he relax? "I'll let you into a secret, Wales is where I relax. I love the tranquillity and peace of the Welsh countryside. My sister lives in Wales and I have been lucky enough to take my family there for the last two Christmases. The wonderful combination of family, fun and fresh air is what relaxation is about for me."

www.petergabriel.com

Bag a Seat

When you go for a walk in the countryside, pop a plastic bag in your pocket so you can sit on it and 'have a whiff' on the grass, a log, or a big stone, if it's damp or wet. Take time to notice what's around you and appreciate your surroundings – using all your senses. Dogs will also thank you for an opportunity to have a sniff and explore in their own time; we often chastise them for stopping and sniffing and 'holding us up' but it's a natural behaviour and it's important for them to enjoy their time out too.

Did you Know?

That the saying 'as cool as a cucumber' originates from the fact that the inside of a cucumber on the vine can be as much as 20 degrees cooler than the outside temperature.

Tom-heart-toes

All Tooled Up

I love my gardening tools, they are like good
friends – they make my life easier and I feel
comfortable with them.

I always buy from Tools for Self Reliance who
refurbish and repair old tools for re-sale in the
UK and also ship them to their partners in Africa
to help them get out of poverty and into work.

The tools are beautiful, the type your
grandparents used to use.

They also have a great range of not-so-well-known tools on
offer – check out the banana planter for example, a multi-
functional tool that also makes a great talking piece!

Lots more details at www.tfsr.org

Love a Duck

Ducks are incredibly sociable creatures and are loved by
many, but did you know that:

- Anatidaephobia is fear of being watched by a duck.

- A group of ducks is called a raft.

- Ducks don't get cold feet as they don't have nerves or
  blood vessels in their feet.

Linnaeus's Floral Clock

Someone said to me recently, "the one thing we all want more of, is time. We are all rushing around as though we are constantly running out of it." I'm not sure that I would want more time actually – I'd only fill that too; surely the secret is to use the time you already have wisely?

Keeping track of the passing of time as well as the seasons has existed for thousands of years. The Chinese, Japanese, Romans, Egyptians, Aztec, Hopi and Navajo Indians, and many others developed various forms of calendars which were all based on Nature. According to Chinese lore, two trees grew at the Emperor's Court. One tree produced a new leaf every day for fifteen days as the moon waxed, and then it shed one leaf every day for fifteen days, as the moon waned. In this way the months were measured. On the other side of the garden was a tree that produced leaves every month for six months, and then shed leaves every month for six months. And so, the passage of years were counted. In the 4th century B.C., Alexander the Great's scribe, Androsthenes, noted that the leaves of certain trees opened during the day and closed at night. In England during the 18th century Tragopogon partensis (Jack-go-to-bed-at-noon) was considered so reliable, that boys working in the fields based their lunchtime on the movement of this flower. In 1729, the French astronomer Jean Jacques d'Ortous deMairan noticed that his heliotrope plant's leaves opened during the day and folded at night (first known experiment on biological rhythms). A Swedish botanist by the name of Carl Linnaeus from University of Uppsala noticed that the flowers of different species opened and closed at certain times each day. It is said that in 1748 he decided to plant a flower clock, so that those who visited him could look at it and tell what hour it was. Others say that Linnaeus probably never actually planted a 'flower clock', but instead based his conclusion on his observations. Either way, he published his findings in "Philosophica Botanica" in 1751.

Linnaeus's Three Groups of Flowers are: *Meteorici* - Flowers which change their opening and closing times according to weather conditions. *Tropici* - Flowers which change their times for opening and closing with the length of the day. *Aequinoctales* - Flowers which have fixed times for opening and closing. Only Aequinoctales are suitable if you want to use flowers to see what time it is.

Linnaeus' Floral Clock
How to tell the *thyme* with flowers; (I couldn't resist!)

2 am   Common Morning Glory (opens) Night-Blooming
       Cereus (closes).

3 am   Imperial Morning Glory (opens 3 - 4 am).

4 am   Yellow Hawkweed (opens at 4.00am), Dog Rose, Chicory,
       Yellow Goats-Beard (opens 4 - 5 am).

5 am   Buttercups, Poppy, Dandelion, Morning Glories, Wild
       Roses (opens 5 - 6 am).

6 am   Spotted Cat's Ear, Potatoes (opens 6 - 7 am).

7 am   African Marigold, Lettuce, White Water Lily (open at 7 am).

8 am   Mouse-Ear Hawkweed, Scarlet Pimpernel, African
       Daisies, Nolana (opens 8 - 9 am) Dandelion (closes 8 - 9 am).

9 am Calendula (Field marigold), Catchfly, Coltsfoot, Gentians,
       Sandworts (opens 9-10 am) Prickly Sow Thistle (closes).

10 am California Poppies (open 10 am -1 pm but only in sunlight)
       Common Nipplewort (closes).

11 am Star-of-Bethlehem (opens at 11 am).

Noon Goatsbeard, Blue Passion flower (opens at noon)
       Morning Glories (closes).

1 pm   Carnation (opens at 1 pm)
       Childing Pink (closes).

2 pm   Afternoon Squill (opens at 2 pm)
       Scarlet Pimpernel, Water Lily (closes) Chicory, Poppy,
       Potatoes, Sandworts (closes 2-3 pm)
       Dandelion (closes 2-5 pm).

3 pm   Hawkbit, Calendula, Spider plant (closes).

4 pm   Purple Hawkweed (opens 4 pm)
       Four O' Clocks (opens 4 - 7 pm)

Small bindweed, Allyssum (closes)
California Poppies, Cat's Ear (closes 4-5 pm).

5 pm   Night-Flowering Catchfly (open 5 - 6 pm) Chicory,
       White Water Lily (closes)
       Coltsfoot (closes 5-6 pm).

6 pm   Showy Evening primrose, Goatsbeard,
       Moonflowers (opens at 6 pm)
       White water lily (closes 6 - 7 pm).

7 pm   White Campion, Fig-marigold (open 7 - 8 pm)
       Iceland poppy, Day Lily, Dog Rose (closes 7-8 pm).

8 pm   Night flowering cereus (open 8 -10 pm) Catchfly,
       Dandelions, Day Lilies (closes 8 -9 pm).

9 pm   Flowering Tobacco (opens 9 -10 pm).

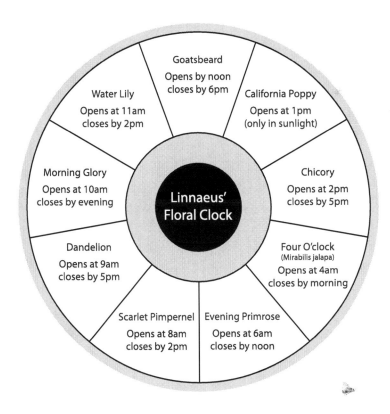

Celebrity Chit-Chat with Radio 2's Terry Walton

I have joined forces with Radio 2's gardener, Terry Walton, several times on radio and to work as a 'double-act' providing talks to various groups and charity events. He is always great company and has shared tales from his own 'gardening path' with me.

"I started gardening when I was 4 yrs old," he told me. "Dad gave me a little patch of soil of my own, next to the shed on his allotment. It was in the 1950's, when men did the gardening in three piece suits.

"By the time I was 15 years old I had 10 plots; it was the 1960's, supermarkets were a novelty and everyone wanted to buy their veg from there; no one wanted an allotment. You're not allowed to sell produce from an allotment, so on a Friday night after school, I would go and collect the wooden tomato trays from the grocers in Tonypandy and fill them with what I'd grown. I had 35 customers who had the veg for nothing but paid a pound for the box it was in," he laughed.

In his early 20's Terry got married to the lovely Anthea and his Allotment Empire diminished. "I kept Dad's two plots and then in the early 90's I went down to just the one plot and it's provided us with produce all year every year since," he claimed proudly. "In the winter we use stored onions and potatoes, the chest freezer is filled with runner beans and broad beans and the garden provides leeks, parsnips, Swedes and Brussels sprouts. April and May are the hardest months to produce food," he said, "although we are still eating our own veg, it's not fresh, it's out of the freezer. I'm not a 'forager' so, apart from black berries, I don't pick food from the hedgerows. All our food comes from the allotment. And I've never been very confident picking mushrooms." he confided, "I'm afraid I'll pick the wrong ones."

Something Terry is confident with is composting and recycling. "I use a kitchen waste fermenter; it lives on the kitchen cupboard and is emptied onto the compost heap every 6 or 7 weeks; it's a brilliant activator." The King of Compost explained, "The Bakashi means you can even put meat and bread in it and it's completely odourless. I also put peelings and shreddings in my wormery and recycle all our paper, glass and tins. I have always recycled; in gardening you do it naturally. A broken bamboo stick will be cut up into 1 ft pieces for row markers and the green house on my allotment is a recycled Second World War pre-fab. As a kid I remember collecting bracken to recycle as compost and horse manure from the pit ponies in the mines was recycled as fertiliser on the allotments."

And it's not just vegetables that Terry grows." I love sweet peas and always grow them up on the allotment; they have great scent, the aphids are attracted to their tips which makes them easy to deal with, they attract other insects which benefit the garden and last but not least, if I'm going to be late home I pick a bunch for Anthea to avoid being in the dog house."

Simply Stunning

A client recently asked for a border to be planted soley with Alchemilla mollis (Lady's Mantle) and Centranthus (Red Valerian) as she had seen the combination in a friend's garden. Both plants are often frowned on by many gardeners for their invasive tendencies, but their enthusiasm for life means they are incredibly easy to grow in any aspect, and need very little attention. They also provide effective ground cover and make great cut flowers. Whether in a vase or in a border, this is a winning combination. Thanks Lizzie H!

Talking to the Plants

A recent advertisement for a gardener on Buckingham Palace's website read "must be able to improve conversation practices". Instead of requesting someone who could improve 'conservation practices', the typing error left applicants wondering if they, like Prince Charles, were going to be talking to the plants.

Berried Treasure

There are many superstitions and legends connected with popular autumnal berries. In one old proverb they signify haste. A man is so excited to pick blackberries that he jumps into the bush and the thorns cause him to lose his eyesight. He regains it upon jumping back out of the bush.

Greek mythology contains a legend similar to this. When Bellerophon, a mortal, tries to ride Pegasus to Olympus, he falls and becomes blind and injured upon landing in a thorny bush. This is his punishment for trying to take the power of the gods. Therefore, the fruit has also come to symbolizes arrogance.

Today I think that haste means we are often missing out on such a rewarding pursuit.

Admittedly, whereas I enjoy the walk and harvest, some batches are now passed onto Mum to actually create the tart, crumble or blackberry vodka. But I have experimented with less traditional recipes, like blackberry sauce (allegedly delicious with pigeon, though as a vegetarian I can vouch that it's also good with char-grilled veggies) and blackberry mustard which is also fabulous as an accompaniment for lots of foods.

And whilst I appreciate some of the technological advances such as Google, I do wish that 'Blackberry' was in prime position in the Google listings as a fruit not a mobile phone!

Blackberries were also used in Christian art to symbolise spiritual neglect or ignorance. Mid-Mediterranean folklore claims Christ's Crown of Thorns was made out of blackberry runners with the deep red juice of the berries representing Christ's blood.

Another legend suggests that the Devil spits (or even pees) on blackberries on Michaelmas Day (29th September) rending them unsuitable for picking. The tale goes that the Devil was kicked out of Heaven on St Michael's Feast Day and landed on a blackberry bush. He cursed the bush and this curse is renewed every year on Michaelmas Day, resulting in the belief it is unlucky to pick blackberries after this date.

If indeed you find it a 'devil' of a job picking the fruit from the thorny bushes, you can grow the thorn-less blackberry in your own garden on trellis work, against a wall or in an informal hedgerow. Choose 'Loch Maree' for beautiful double pink flowers which make the shrub attractive as well as productive, or the 'Loch Ness' variety that is perfect for the smaller garden and doesn't need staking. Both varieties fruit well and are disease resistant.

And the last words must go to American author and farmer, with a relevant surname, Wendell Berry, who advises,

"Better than any argument,
is to rise at dawn and pick
dew-wet berries."

Cutting the (Blackberry) Mustard

4 oz blackberries (or raspberries), finely chopped
1 1/2 tablespoons whole-grain mustard
2 teaspoons honey

Mash blackberries (or raspberries), mustard and honey in a small bowl until it looks like a chunky sauce.

Minty Mint-Tea

Rather than let mint take over beds and borders, grow it in tubs or even window boxes and hanging baskets.

Like all herbs, it is best to pick often to encourage new and bushy growth, so pick your mint every morning for a zesty wake-up cuppa.

Leave the crushed leaves to infuse in boiling water before drinking and add a little honey to sweeten if necessary.

A squeeze of lemon will act as a great detox and a little grated ginger will energise.

Children are for people who can't have dogs

Animal's Wise and Wild Ways

I have been fortunate enough to work with the fabulous Caroline Ingraham who is renowned in the animal world for pioneering the study of domestic animals self-medicating with herbs and plants.

Known as Zoopharmacognosy, Caroline explained, "It's is the oldest therapy on the Planet; its where life began. If left to our own devices we would be able to heal ourselves naturally and many wild animals still do."

Caroline began her career training with the great Robert Tisserand in the use of essential oils and their uses.
"I was extremely impressed by the effects of the oils and in particular when I was cured from recurring cystitis with a few drops of Juniper in hot water.

"I later rescued a really ill dog from Battersea Dogs Home; she hadn't eaten for days and the vet wanted to put her to sleep. I had never treated an animal with the oils but massaged Frankincense into her belly and within an hour she was eating. She made a full recovery as did another dog I had that got bitten by a Rattle Snake in California. The snake bite caused massive internal bleeding which is often fatal. My dog was bleeding heavily from the nose and I gave him carrot seed oil as I knew studies had proven it reduced blood loss. Immediately the blood slowed to a slow drip and by administering more at regular intervals, he too made a full recovery." "The oils are simply miracles in a bottle," she added passionately.

And it's not only domestic animals that the dedicated animal lover has treated. "The Sheltered Trust (as seen on the Elephant Diaries on BBC TV) asked me to fly out and treat a very sick elephant for them. I had to go immediately as the vet was planning on putting her down the very next day. She had fallen into a putrid water well and had the most horrific injuries that had also gone septic. Hyenas had mutilated her trunk and she was in shock. Elephants can only have two courses of antibiotics due to possible complications, so there was nothing more the vet could do for her. I put green clay on the wounds which dried them up, drew the bad stuff out and kept the flies off. The elephant also selected huge quantities of garlic essential oil to boost her immune system. The vet gave her a reprieve that very afternoon. Five days later, she was playing with a stick and the wounds healed completely within 11 days."

So what is the difference between plants eaten for food and plants eaten for medicine? "If an animal eats vegetation for calorific effect," answered Caroline, "the food is stored as fat or energy; the body retains food. If a plant is eaten for medicinal purposes, as soon as it has done its job the body detoxes it to prevent poisoning.

All animals know instinctively what they need to feel better and to maintain good health and will therefore select their own oils or plants. They also know the correct individual dosage they need, which is why we shouldn't add the supplements to their food bowl. We need to remember and respect how our four-legged friends would have lived in the wild; dogs often drink from muddy puddles as they need the algae in the water. Despite being domesticated, animals are still intuitively able to identify the plants chemicals they need for perfect health and the hedgerows are simply Nature's Medicine cabinet!"

Find out more about Caroline's courses, case studies and the books she has written at www.ingraham.co.uk

Cat-a-tonic?

Catnip, (Nepeta cataria) is a member of the mint family and one of the most popular plants for cats to self medicate with. It can act both as a stimulant and a sedative depending on what the cat needs. Cats will roll around on the plant crushing the leaves and inhaling the aroma. If inhaled it will raise the heartbeat and 'excite' but if chewed it will have a sedative effect.

If you have a 'house cat' put some sprigs of catmint in a clean litter tray for the cat to enjoy. Two thirds of cats react with a pseudo narcotic effect which is hereditary.

A Matter of Taste

A horrified mother saw her little boy about to put a slug in his mouth and shrieked "don't do that, it won't taste very nice." The little boy proceeded to eat the small slug, shrugged and replied, "tastes just like worms."

Just Say No

Saying 'No' to wasps, has proven surprisingly effective for me of late. I was told that insects actually understand the words, or intention, Yes and No and obviously a stern 'No' at the appropriate time is a far kinder option to swatting and squishing them! So when I found a large wasp nest just inside the entrance of my tool shed – a shed I used most days -it seemed the perfect opportunity to try the theory. I addressed the nest:

"I am told that you understand the word 'NO'; so I am prepared to let you stay here as long as you do not sting or intimidate me, my dog or any visitors. If you do, then I will destroy your home immediately and any others I find nearby."

Throughout the summer months I entered the shed passing under the busy nest most days and reminded them of our 'deal' and adding a stern 'No' if they got a bit excited. I also had three other nests around the cottage and repeated the warning to each nest, making it clear that if one wasp from any of the nests violated our agreement I would destroy them all. No one, nor my inquisitive terrier, was stung and we all went about our day-to-day stuff without bothering each other.

During the early autumn the queens leave the nests looking for somewhere to overwinter and suddenly the remaining workers have no focus and nothing to do. That coincides with fruit windfalls and the workers tend to go and get drunk, getting notoriously bad tempered, looking for trouble. But even then we lived in relative harmony – I raised my voice occasionally but that was it. Needless to say, I will be trying the same approach next year.

Stiff Stalks

Scientists in Australia originally discovered Viagra's plant preserving qualities and the research was published in the British Medical Journal (BMJ) stating, *"Viagra can double the shelf life of cut flowers; you only need a tiny amount of Viagra to stiffen things up nicely."*

Apparently, just 1 mg (there are 50mg in a single tablet) dissolved into water with your plants will make them last a week longer.

Viagra contains nitric oxide which slows down the dying process in plants and now scientists are working on ways to market a gardeners' version of Viagra for plants.

Not got any Viagra? Then soluble aspirin also works in the same way, too. Put one tablet into some wilting flowers and the effervescence will prolong their life.

Cinnamon can be used as a substitute for rooting hormone. It also kills fungus and bacteria at the same time.

Purifying Plants

I have rekindled my love affair with house plants after working with Singing Plants and also including them in my Green Rooms. I hadn't realised that they had become quite so out-of-fashion. Sadly it seems that a lot of people prefer not to have them in the house as they find them 'messy' and tiresome to keep watered. It's worth the effort as they are actually hardworking. In the late '80's, NASA and the Associated Landscape Contractors of America studied houseplants as a way to purify the air in space facilities. They found several plants that filter out common volatile organic compounds (VOCs).

We are exposed to a range of indoor air contaminants daily, including, smoke, toxins, chemicals off-gassing, pesticides, detergent fumes, mold, small fibres, bacteria etc. Plants act as filters because they absorb the toxins through their leaves, especially those with the largest leaves. The theory is that if the plants do the absorbing first, our nose and lungs take on less of a burden. That means reduced incidence of asthma, allergies, reactions to mold and other particles, and immunosuppressed illnesses. Rooms that benefit most from the addition of plants are those that are heavily laden with electrical equipment, such as studies and TV rooms and of course all offices.

Some of the most efficient 'air filters' are:
- Dwarf date palm
- Boston fern
- Peace Lily
- English ivy
- Rubber plant
- Weeping fig
- Christmas cactus
- Spider plant

Sow 'n' Go

After seeing some innovative planting ideas over the years I love what I have termed the 'sow and go' method – you simply sow your seeds and then go and do something else far more interesting than faffing over them, until harvest time. Plants want to grow – they don't need lovely neat square beds or boxes to do so.

I have become more and more endeared by people who are both proactive and creative in their garden; like the couple who were renovating their new house and didn't have time to create the veg patch of their dreams so in the meantime, they used the builder's bulk bags to grow potatoes, courgettes and tomatoes.

Like the old farmer who can no longer tend his veggie area so he simply ploughs two furrows at the top of one of his fields to grow his own spuds, his favourite.

Or the lady who has downsized from her grand abode where she had a full-time gardener and now grows her own veggies in pots on her patio.

Good gardeners are not obsessed by organising nature, they simply 'grow with the flow!'.

Wild Life v Lazy Life

Stingy nettles and brambles are now in the top ten most common countryside plants. These, and other 'enthusiastic' plants like ivy and bindweed, are strangling the prettier, low growing wild flowers, a recent survey has found. In 1990 the bramble was the 14th most common plant now it's at number 7. The nettle has gone from 11th to 5th pushing out plants like broadleaved willowherb, marsh valerian and the delicate harebells. Cutting back nettles regularly will also encourage the growth of new young nettles tops for curries and soups! So, don't take the 'wildlife' gardening concept too far and neglect to manage relevant areas sensibly. Responsible 'wildlife' gardening is quite different from letting your garden turn into a wilderness.

The Original Celtic Year

Imbolc: 1st February	Lughnasa: 1st August
Beltaine: 1st May	Samhain: 1st November

Celebrity Chit-Chat with the Hairy Bikers

The Hairy Bikers, Dave Myers and Si King have recently become the Hairy Dieters by losing over 6 stone between them. The food loving bikers changed their eating habits and created low fat versions of some of our most popular dishes, such as skinny lasagne, as documented on the BBC's series, The Hairy Dieters. Their new cookbook, How to Love Food and Lose Weight, knocked E L James's erotic trilogy, 50 Shades of Grey off the top of Amazon's best-sellers list.

"We've always known our food is sexy but this is mad," said the Bikers. "Sex may be important but the way to a nation's heart is still through its stomach. We're delighted and thrilled that people have taken the programme in the spirit in which it was intended. You can still have a pint and enjoy your food."

"We are definitely leaner and greener than when we were in Wales last," explained Dave, referring to a previous Food Tour of Britain.

"We love Wales; the strong cultural identity is followed through in the Welsh food. And you've got everything – great Welsh Black beef in the fields, tasty Welsh lamb on the hills, Sewin in the rivers and even cockles on the coasts. Though I think my favourite is probably laver bread."

Si disagreed. "It's an acquired taste," he mused, "though I've noticed the Welsh have got a salty tooth. I'm more of a beach forager myself and love sea beet.

Though, we both enjoy foraging blackberries and sloes from the hedgerows too."

"With gin or vodka," Dave laughed. "Although we love eating and cooking, neither of us have got around to growing our own food yet. I live on a small island so all I can grow is mildew."

The hilarious double act continues as Si confessed, "My wife's dead good at growing stuff, it might not be what I want but it's nice anyway. We are about to buy a plot so she can grow more. I did grow some leeks once but whilst I was away she turned it into a herb bed."

"I think it's important to focus on what you do best," said Dave wisely, "and for us that's cooking, eating, biking, travelling and talking rubbish."

"We do that so well," agreed Si, adding "98% of good cooking is about good shopping or sourcing good food. Local produce is always better and we discovered some terrific Welsh flavours that we didn't expect, like the charcuterie from Triley and the Welsh mead."

The Welsh are clever," said Dave, "they do lots of nice takes on traditional food. I think my favourite might be the Welsh Black fillet," he added.

"Three quick tips for cooking it," added Si. "Never cook straight from the fridge; only turn it twice whilst cooking (it stretches otherwise) and leave it to relax for a bit before you eat it."

www.hairybikers.com

Dog's Dinner

Thank you to TV vet Joe Inglis for sharing a recipe from his Pets Kitchen; for others visit www.petskitchen.co.uk

This is definitely Yogi's (my West Highland Terrier-ist) favourite -
Meaty Parsnip Mash.
The ingredients are:

- 250g stewing steak, diced. 1 teaspoon oil
- A couple of medium potatoes (around 350g)
- A couple of parsnips (around 200g)
- A carrot
- A teaspoon of Marmite
- 100g grated cheddar cheese

Wash the veg thoroughly but don't peel them as this removes a lot of the goodness. Put it all together into a pan of boiling water and let it simmer for about 15 minutes – until it's all quite soft. Fry up the diced steak in the oil. Don't worry about cooking it all the way through – dogs love rare meat. Mash up all the cooked veg, then mix in the Marmite, cheese and fried steak. Mix it all together and let it cool. Serve on its own or mixed in with some dried biscuits.

Keep Off, Cats

I recently heard that that water retaining gel granules will deter cats from beds and borders as they just don't like the jelly-like substance. Simply sprinkle the gel crystals on the surface of the soil and wait for rain, or sprinkle with water, to activate the gel reaction.

No Place like Gnome

The word 'gnome' derives from the Latin word 'gnomus', meaning 'earth-dweller' as it was thought they used to live underground.

The first known gnomes were made of clay and produced in Germany in the early 1800's. They were introduced to the garden to bring good luck and guard crops.

Keep ON the Grass

In 1625, Sir Francis Bacon wrote, "nothing is more pleasant to the eye than green grass closely shorn." Not only are lawned areas great to look at but they're good for our health too.

Turfed areas absorb carbon dioxide and trap pollution, prevent excessive rain run-off and release oxygen, improving the air that we breathe. On a hot summers day a lawn will be approx 30 degrees cooler than tarmac and 15 degrees cooler than bare soil. Grassed areas can also reduce noise by up to 30%.

Lawn Rangers

In the 16th and 17th century, overseas visitors marvelled at the British lawn. It would take three skilled scythe-men a whole day to cut an acre of grass and women, known as 'lawn women' would work behind them brushing up the shorn grass.

Take a Plant for a Pint

Research carried out in Russia shows that plants do in fact have emotions.

Although this concept is met with frank incredulity by mainstream scientists and thinkers who believe that emotions requires a central nervous system, made up of nerves and a brain, the Bengali scientist Sir Jagadis Chandra Bose suggests that in the same way that plants breathe, eat and move without the aid of lungs, gills, stomach or muscles – why could they not feel without a brain or nerves?

Bose showed how plants reacted to stimuli such as touch poison and heat in the same way animal nerves-plus-muscle responded.

He was even able to measure reactions to alcohol that resembled drunkenness.

Many Moons

In myth and folklore the full moon of each month is given a name. There are many variations, but the following list gives the most widely known names:

January Wolf Moon, After Yule, Ice Moon, Old Moon

February Snow Moon, Hunger Moon, Storm Moon, Candles Moon

March Storm Moon, Crow Moon, Crust Moon, Sugar Moon, Sap Moon, Chaste Moon, Death Moon, Worm Moon, Lenten Moon

April Growing Moon, Sprouting Grass Moon, Fish Moon, Growing Moon, Waking Moon, Pink Moon

May Flower Moon, Corn Planting Moon, Corn Moon, Hare Moon, Flower Moon

June Mead Moon Honey Moon, Rose Moon, Hot Moon, Planting Moon, Flower Moon, Strawberry Moon

July Hay Moon, Thunder Moon, Mead Moon

August Corn Moon, Red Moon, Green Grain Moon, Lightning Moon, Dog Moon

September Harvest Moon, Corn Moon, Barley Moon, Fruit Moon

October Hunter's Moon, Travel Moon, Dying Grass Moon, Blood Moon, Harvest Moon

November Beaver Moon, Frost Moon, Snow Moon, Hunter's Moon

December Winter Moon, Frost Moon, Winter Moon, Long Night's Moon, Moon Before Yule

Chocs Away

For choco-holic gardener's the Cosmos atrosanguineus or 'chocolate cosmos', will be a real treat. The gorgeous velvety maroon blooms really do smell of chocolate - although are not edible. Seeds of the tender perennial can be sown outdoors in March for 'scent-sational' blooms later in the year.

Did You know ...?

Cacao (or cocoa) beans were also once used as money. 100 beans could buy a slave or a rabbit would cost 4 beans, so money did 'grow on trees'.

And the great Joan Rivers knows the power of chocolate, "My therapist told me I would feel better if I finished things; so far today I have finished a bag of Maltesers, a Twix and a box of After Eights and I feel better all ready."

Tasty Buds

Edible flowers have regained popularity recently and many of them can also be crystallised for that extra special touch (or crunch).

Little viola flowers are probably the easiest and safest to start with and Sarah Hughes of www.eatmyflowers.co.uk has been kind enough to pass on her basic method.

- Beat fresh egg whites lightly (use pasteurised egg whites if you are going to do a lot)
- Paint gently onto flowers
- Then cover in caster sugar and let them dry.

Commercially, Sarah's flowers have a four-month shelf life although I'm sure you won't be able to resist your homemade goodies for that long.

Gone To Pot

Most plastic flowerpots are made from polypropylene which few recycling outlets accept so try the following ideas for reusing:

- Fill partially with sand and use as an outdoor ashtray (covering the drainage holes first)
- Use as a scoop for compost or pet food
- Use for collecting chicken eggs or fruit and veg
- Use larger pots for storage - kids toys, rags, cleaning products
- Use as waste paper bins (putting a plastic bag inside will recycle those too)
- Put over a bird feeder to deter squirrels

No Need To Pardon Your Garden

I often get asked for relatively quick, easy and cost effective ways to revamp a garden or at least areas of a garden.

At the risk of sounding a little trite, the first step is always to tidy it up! Have a good clear up; remove old broken flower pots, children's toys which aren't being used and any piles of rubbish that have just built up as they have a tendency to do.

Then cut back anything that is overgrown – hedges, shrubs that are blocking pathways, branches overhanging paths or which make mowing awkward, and out-of-control climbers. Next, remove or repair anything that is broken or just looks tatty, be it repairing fence panels, re-hanging garden gates or removing old and broken trellis work, for example.

These three simple steps will usually make a huge difference for the minimum investment – maybe just a few trips to the tip and your time.

Then you are ready for the exciting stuff. I am a huge advocate of paint in the garden. I love seeing fences, sheds, benches, arbours, trellis work painted but not that awful 'Ground Force blue' that gave garden paint such a bad name. There are some fantastic paints and colours on the market now and some DIY stores are even able to mix a colour to your exact requirement. Just always make sure it is suitable for outdoor application – and whether it is suitable for wood or masonry.

The paint company Bedec, are a fabulous find. Their Multi Purpose Paint will cover any outdoor (or indoor) surface without primer or undercoat. I have seen plastic patio furniture, flower pots, fences, railings, sheds and summer houses and even pet hutches and runs totally transformed by their easy to use, one-coat Multi Purpose Paint. They also have a fabulous range of colours to choose from, whether you are looking for something subtle and peaceful – lights greens, creams, soft blues and neutral colours or wanting to jazz up your space or furniture with funkier, more vibrant colours.

Be imaginative, be brave and have some fun – and make sure you have a couple of paint brushes to hand as once you start you won't want to stop!

Copper Load of Slugs!

One of the questions I get asked the most at gardening related events is how to deter slugs and snails. I started using copper tools in my own garden a couple of years ago and have had no problems with slugs since. It's a big claim to make (and just to make you feel better, I still battle with other pests and diseases) but I believe copper to be the best deterrent. I also have lengths of copper pipe randomly placed in various beds and I soak copper pipe in watering cans of water to water plants with when necessary.

Apparently slug slime reacts with copper to give slugs a little electric shock if they come into contact with it and I think it's this aversion to copper which just makes them uneasy around the stuff, therefore they will slide off to eat in a more relaxed environment. Wouldn't you choose to eat without the risk of an electric shock with every mouthful?

Copper is believed to deter a number of insects. Putting copper tape above an outside door, or even using copper pennies, is also thought to keep flies out of the house.

Other 'slug swervers' I believe work, include incorporating parsley and cosmos into vulnerable beds and borders.

I have grown parsley as a low border around a flower bed of hostas as an experiment and it worked; cosmos is such a beautiful addition to any border I recommend growing them whether you have a slug problem or not.

Slugs don't like mint, tansy, fennel or rosemary either, so planting these may help.

Ducks are great slug-slayers but unless you have a suitable habitat for them, they will cause more mess and damage than the slugs themselves. Of course encouraging toads and hedgehogs into your garden is proving a Slug Patrol as nature intended.

I have been told 'coffee kills snails and slugs quite well,', though I'm not sure if it is possible to be killed 'quite well' – apparently it can be sprayed around plants, on leaves, or directly on the molluscs themselves. Research by the USDA in Hawaii showed that a 1 to 2 percent caffeine solution killed slugs and snails within two days.

Used coffee grinds are also being trialled as an organic deterrent and coffee is also a stimulant for plants, as well as people, so an added bonus is increased plant growth.

Other methods I have heard of but will leave to you to ponder or trial, include putting glue onto fallen leaves and then sprinkling with salt, putting dog and cat hair or talcum powder around vulnerable plants and probably the strangest .... garlic mash!

The above are best avoided if you have pets.

"Never mind
Knick-Knack-Paddy-Whack,
just get to the good bit!"

Celebrity Chit-Chat with Bill Tidy

Cartoonist Bill Tidy admits that he was in his 40's before he 'decided to grow things'. He explained, "I never bothered with gardening before that – apart from the lawn. I loved a striped lawn, it was my forte."

Also well known for his written work, (Bill has written 20 books and illustrated 70) and broadcasting, he told me proudly, "We've got quite a big garden and once I started, I did very well. I even developed our paddock into a vegetable garden which looked amazing until about 4 years ago. Now the weeds have drifted in and taken over. I'm frightened to go in there now, it's probably turned into a Rhubarb Forest."

Bill explained what happened. "I grew brussels sprouts for the first time and was quite excited, until one morning I went out to find all the plants had been completely stripped by something pesky overnight. It was a major blow; I was left with a little row of skeletons. I thought, I don't mind sharing some of my veg with the wildlife but to take them all was bad sportsmanship. It really set me back.

"We've got a small greenhouse that's got a bit of everything in it and I grow most of our veg in pots now. I've grown fabulous artichokes and courgettes in pots and my wife Rosa cooks the flowers with a raspberry sauce. They are delicious, I could just keep eating them.

"We've also raised two figs this year. I looked after them

like children, but the birds still managed to have one of them. I've netted my blackcurrants though," he added, "they're not having those."

Well known for drawing as fast as he speaks, Bill is happy to adopt a slower pace in the garden. "I give all my plants time and talk to them all" he admitted. "Only yesterday I had to chastise the tomatoes plants as they were dropping the tomatoes and they had been eaten before I could get to them. I had to tell them to hang on".

"It's been a really good growing year," continued the cartoonist, "Runner beans are like a currency around here; people take little bundles of them to the pub and trade them he laughed. "I love them too."

"I think raspberries are my favourite, though, they're so persistent and taste so good. And potatoes are very rewarding too. You can even grow them in sacks now.

"It all helps as I don't have to bend down so far. My hands are as steady as they were when I was 20 but the rest of me is a bit creaky! What I need is a sort of guillotine style platform that I can lie full length on and hover just above the ground to avoid bending to do the garden. Perhaps I'll sketch you something?"

And bless him, he did.

www.billtidy.com

Super Seed

Seed companies are promising 'super seeds' for the future; the Digitalis 'Illumination' shouldn't even exist according to botanists, although gardeners will be glad it does, it's gorgeous and quite exotic looking; the nasturtium 'Flame Thrower' is another first with serrated petals and a strong fragrance not normally associated with nasturtiums and 'Orange Troika' is a superb new trailing nasturtium that also provides great ground cover; the lettuce 'Lettony' has been bred to cope with our erratic British summer and resists both bolting and rotting; and there are even stripy courgettes (Sunstripe) and black peas (Mange Tout Shiraz) to encourage you to grow your own.

Go Wild

It seems wildflower meadows and drifts are still vogue and I often get asked for my advice and/or help in creating an area of wild flowers within an existing garden. It is not always the particularly low maintenance, or cost effective, option that most people imagine it to be and many people are disappointed, and even disbelieving, when I explain it's not as easy or straight forward as nature makes it look.

Good quality seed is essential and wildflowers prefer poor soil which means that occasionally top soil has to be removed. They can take a while to become established if having to compete with strong grasses or conversely can flourish in the first year only to disappoint in subsequent years. That said, when done properly, the results can be stunning and well worth the investment of time and money. For smaller areas in your garden I recommend planting little 9cm pots of taller alpines and small herbaceous varieties like the eye catching Geums, Verbascums, and Achilleas amongst the more traditional wild flowers for more impact and interest.

Discussing this idea with the wonderful and wise Neil McDonald, of McDonalds Nurseries in Abergavenny during one of our many put-the world-to-right chats, we agreed this type of planting should be called 'Pseudo Wildflowers'.

It could catch on!

Cut Your Own

The latest gardening trend is growing your own cut flowers, and seems to be seems to be taking over from the recent surge of people growing their own veg. I have also seen a shift away from growing your own veggies as people are finding it too difficult and time consuming.

A lot of people who have gone to the trouble of creating raised beds and little veggie patches in their garden are a little despondent at the thought of all that work and money going to waste.

If this sounds familiar, don't despair – use these cultivated areas to grow flowers 'en mass' and use them as cut flowers for the house, or just to add colour and interest in the garden. Sow annuals like the fabulous cosmos, marigolds and snapdragons and add a few edible flowers like nasturtium and calendula too, to cheer up the wildlife, the gardener, the house and even the cook.

Doing Porridge

I discovered the extra energy boost that porridge can provide during my time as a marathon runner but of course you don't have run marathons in order to benefit from the slow release energy effect of a good healthy breakfast.

Here are my two favourite versions, the first is for 'fat porridge' and the second one is 'skinny porridge'; you'll see why.

Either make your porridge using full fat milk and/or a little cream. Stir in desiccated coconut and brown sugar and serve with maple syrup.

Or soak your porridge oats in a little water over night and cook with a few crushed cardamom seeds cinnamon and chopped dates and drizzle with honey to serve.

Homemade Energy Soup

Ingredients :

- A handful of mixed sprouts - mung beans, green peas, lentils for example (not the leafy brassica!).
- A large handful of indoor greens, such as sunflower greens and buckwheat lettuce, watercress, parsley.
- A handful of peeled apples or watermelon.

Simply blend (heat gently if preferred) and enjoy.

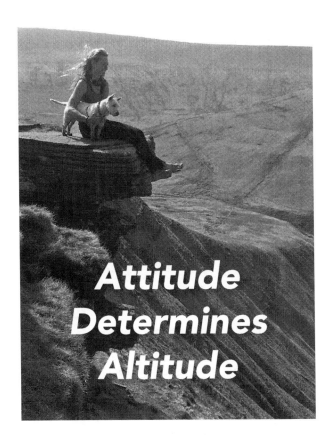

Attitude Determines Altitude

Green Rooms

One of my recent endeavours has been installing Green Rooms and Green Spaces into work places and schools. It is basically bringing aspects and elements of the outdoors inside to create a pleasant and productive indoor environment which helps improve wellbeing and therefore reduce employee sick days.

It is a very effective way to improve the mood and relationships between colleagues and also employees and clients, as well as improving children's interactions and behaviour in schools.

There are several methods and elements which are used to promote harmony in the workplace and one of the simplest is remarked upon often as being particularly therapeutic, and that is background bird song.

We take it for granted outdoors as it lifts the spirits subconsciously but it is easy to recreate the benefits indoors by using a CD of pre-recorded bird song.

It is incredibly relaxing and calming. I often use it when I am working at my computer and in an era where tweeting means something different to a certain age group, I highly recommend trying the 'original' tweeters.

I bet you find it more relaxing than the more recent version.

Little Victories

"One day you'll meet yourself coming back!" is what my Nan used to tell me, as I have always had a tendency to be busy.

Occasionally though, enthusiasm morphs into overwhelm and whilst working with my ever-calm brother during one of my exhausted phases I asked, "Why don't you ever seem to get overwhelmed with things?"

"It's easy," he shrugged, "I just break all the things I've got to do down into little jobs, like bite-sized pieces; then when they're done, I tick them off and each one becomes a little victory! Every little victory you make inspires you to make another ... just repeat!"

HSP's

If 'overwhelm' is a word you are familiar with then you may be a Highly Sensitive Person.

Psychotherapist and author Elaine Aron began researching high sensitivity in 1991 and has defined a distinct personality trait that affects as many as one out of every five people. According to Dr. Aron's definition, the Highly Sensitive Person (HSP) has a sensitive nervous system, is aware of subtleties in his/her surroundings, and is more easily overwhelmed when in a highly stimulating environment.

- Are you easily overwhelmed by such things as bright lights, strong smells, coarse fabrics, or sirens?
- Do you make a point of avoiding violent movies and TV shows?
- Do you need to withdraw during busy days, into bed or a darkened room or some other place where you can have privacy and relief from the situation?
- Do you make it a high priority to arrange your life to avoid upsetting or overwhelming situations?

Dr. Aron explains that in the past HSPs have been called "shy," "timid," "inhibited," or "introverted," but these labels completely miss the nature of the trait. Thirty percent of HSPs are actually extraverts. HSPs only appear inhibited because they are so aware of all the possibilities in a situation. They pause before acting, reflecting on their past experiences.

Sensitivity is anything but a flaw.

Many HSPs are often unusually creative and productive workers, attentive and thoughtful partners, and intellectually gifted individuals. Find out more at www.hsperson.com

'Ion' it Out

Numerous studies continue to prove that fresh air is beneficial to our health, mentally, physically and emotionally It appears that whilst most people are aware of the benefits of being outdoors many are still not spending enough time

simply taking in the fresh air and enjoying
natural elements and surroundings. One of the
reasons being outdoors boosts our wellbeing
is because the atmosphere is made up of
negative and positive air ions – the positive ions
are bad for us and the negative ions are good
for us.

Confused? Don't be, just think posions = pos-ions.
Positive ions are found hanging around in many offices
and buildings, particularly around fluorescent lighting,
computers, mobile phones and other techy equipment.
They will contribute to operators feeling lethargic and even
unwell.

Negative ions, (the ones that are good for us) on the other
hand, are found in abundance in the fresh air, around water,
at the top of mountains, in woods and forest, at the seaside
and around plants and grassed areas.

This is one of the reasons we feel so much better after
visiting these places.

So whether you go and buy yourself a beautiful houseplant
for your desk at work, carry a precious pebble in your
pocket or go and walk by a wonderful waterfall – aim to do
something to reacquaint yourself with nature and feel the
benefits.

Bouncing Berries

When John "Peg-Leg" Webb poured a load of cranberries down his storage-loft stairs as his wooden leg made it impossible to carry them, he noticed that the firmest and the finest bounced to the bottom and the bruised and spoiled lingered on the upper steps.

He realized then that the fruit's "bounceability" was the perfect test to separate the good from the bad.

That was in 1880 but today the bounce test is still used to make sure the best berries make it to the store.

Try it for yourself.

Core! Did you know?

- Pomology is the science of apple growing.
- Apples are a member of the rose family.
- It takes energy from 50 leaves to produce one apple.
- To keep potatoes fresh and prevent sprouting, put an apple in the bag.
- In recipes calling for white wine, you can use apple juice.
- Fresh apples float because 25% of their volume is air.
- Cold storage technology means that the apple you are eating in this year could have been harvested last year.

Celebrity Chit-Chat with Dara Ó Briain

I met comedian and TV presenter Dara Ó Briain for lunch at the Hay Festival and it's fair to say that he visibly squirmed when the conversation turned to gardening.

"I have the same sort of interest in my garden as I have in my kitchen appliances," he immediately confessed.

"I inherited both the garden and the appliances with the house; they are functional but I don't have any interest in either of them. I like being in the garden but not to work. I get people in to help out with that. I don't even mow the lawn, my father never did either.

"My only point of interaction with the garden is to pick rosemary to go with a lamb dish occasionally," he grinned, adding "It took me three days to get the sprinklers sorted out recently; one side of the garden was flooded and the other half bone dry. I'm probably responsible for the drought in the south.

"My mother was a professional florist so she obviously loved and appreciated flowers and all I remember about gardening whilst growing up is being told off for kicking a football into the flowerbeds and breaking all the flowers. I appreciate the beauty of flowers and I quite like fruit; I've got a couple of fruit trees in my garden and even a banana tree but none of them ever quite manages to produce any fruit."

'No plans to compete with Fyffes bananas then?' I asked.

"No, but did you know that Fyffes is an Irish company and is the largest importer and exporter of bananas? They buy in all the Costa Rican bananas and then export them." He was suddenly quite animated.

"I learnt that on QI. We were also asked what would we do if I saw a bee dying; the answer was to give it sugar or honey but I said stamp on it to put it out of its misery."

He is completely unrepentant when I share that I'm a beekeeper. "Oh yeah? I keep flies," he retorted, "got a house full of them and a few wasps. I'm not really into all the country stuff; I'm more of a city person."

He continued, "My cat used to catch frogs and there is no noise quite like a frog screaming for its life; the same cat killed a squirrel and hid it in the cupboard once; they are slices of nature I don't miss in the city." He shrugged unapologetically.

Famously unsupportive of holistic medicine and the healing properties of plants, Dara explains, "I've got nothing against plants but let's not go giving them super powers.

"People grab a fragment of science and run with it; they think a metaphor is science. Talking to plants for example, what's that about? Sound is simply a difference in air pressure, plants aren't going to recognise that. It's bull s**t.

"It's true that that there are certain genomes in humans and plants that are the same and 50% of our genes are in common with a banana but it doesn't mean we can have a conversation with them."

www.daraobriain.com

There Are Holes In The Sky
by Spike Milligan

There are holes in the sky
Where the rain gets in
But they're ever so small
That's why the rain is thin

It may be thin but the fastest speed a falling raindrop can hit you is 18mph.

Super Soup

How to curry favour with Curried Pumpkin and Apple Soup

- 2 tablespoons butter
- 1 small chopped onion
- 3 sticks chopped celery
- 1 large apple, peeled, cored, and chopped
- 2 teaspoons mild curry powder or paste
- 1 pint of vegetable stock
- 1 lb (ish) of chopped pumpkin flesh

Melt the butter in saucepan and stir in the onion, celery, pumpkin and apple.

Sauté slowly for about 10 minutes.

Stir in the curry powder and cook gently for another minute or two.

Stir in a third of vegetable stock and simmer for another couple of minutes.

Pour the contents of the pan into a blender or food processor, add the pumpkin, and puree the soup until its smooth.

Pour it all back into the pot, stir in the remaining vegetable stock, season and simmer for 5 minutes.

For a vegan option, substitute butter with a little coconut oil.

Fantastic Franchi

How about growing your own pet food?

Or maybe even growing your own coffee or truffles?
Franchi Seeds have a fabulous range called the Golden Line
Pet Seed Range which have been carefully selected and
formulated by vets to supplement the dietary needs of your
pet.

Not only can you buy seed mixes for your cat which
includes Nepeta Cataria and mixed grasses that aid
digestion, you can choose from mixes of lettuce, veggies,
clover and spinach for your rabbit, hamster or guinea pig
and even seed varieties for your tortoise, parrot or budgie.

It's a clever idea that links to the Zoopharmacognosy that I
practise (how animals self-medicate in the wild) and I love it.

Other innovative ranges include the Le Bizzarre range which
includes 'Coffea Arabica' seeds and even several different
varieties of truffle trees. Their catalogue makes very good
reading and their products very original presents.

www.seedsofitaly.com or call 02084275020 for a catalogue.

"Don't judge each day by the harvest you reap but by
the seeds that you plant."

- Robert Louis Stevenson

Brave New Word

What a fabulous compliment I received recently; I have been given 'verb status'.

A friend's husband has coined the term to be '*Allbutted*'.

Apparently whenever I chat, email, text or actually meet up with Cher, she goes home bubbling over with new ideas and enthusiasm for various endeavours I have shared.

Often without any prior knowledge of our interactions, Tim has noted and remarked that that Cher has obviously '*been Allbutted*'. How wonderful and thank you both for 'Chering'.

Bug Off

After writing about my secret mosquito repellent for a National newspaper, I was inundated with requests wanting to know more.

Whilst living in the Caribbean, I was introduced to the not-so-much-of-a-secret-now body oil that is used by the SAS, fishermen and travellers the world over to repel mozzies, midges, and even horse flies. It is ... drum-roll please ... Avon's Skin So Soft Body Oil (the original formula). It's fabulous; I wouldn't be without it.

Celebrity Chit-Chat **with Francis Rossi**

A big fan of Status Quo, I was thrilled to discover Francis Rossi is a big fan of his garden.

He told me, "I used to live just 100 yards down the road from where we live now and I lived there for over 30 years. The garden was beautiful; it was 3 acres of mature trees and formal Italian gardens, very secluded and well planned out by the previous owners. Now we have just over an acre and have planted loads of things, including 360 laurels, three Indian bean trees, and three Handkerchief trees.
I love laurels, they are so reliable and I love the little vibrant green leaves in the spring. The problem I have is that things just don't grow quick enough. I am determined to live to 100 to see it all mature.

"I remember the droughts of 1976 and being really worried for all my trees. I love to see it rain now 'cos I know it's good for my garden. One of my Handkerchief trees isn't looking very well at the moment so I'll give it some Bach Rescue Remedy.

"I believe in all that homeopathic stuff. I have a great woman who helps me with all the homeopathic and holistic stuff and she told me to give the tree Rescue Remedy.

"I have always suffered from migraines and found the only thing that helps alleviate them is Tongkat Ali. It has a bad press because it is associated with improving men's performance but I have to speak as I find and it works for my migraines. There is so much we don't understand about nature's abilities. We need to learn to trust these old remedies."

As well as being a fan of nature and his garden, Francis obviously loves his animals too. As well as a Westie and a Labrador he also has a pet pigeon, Sid, who was rescued by his daughter Keira Tallulah.

"Sid's tapping on the window," he explained halfway through our chat, "Can you hold on while I go and get him some food?"

Francis has eight children and affectionately refers to them by numbers; "Kid no. 1 loves his garden but he has a lot of help and kid no. 3 is keen too; he's copied me by planting loads of laurels. All the kids appreciate a nice garden though because they grew up in one.

"Eileen (Francis's wife) loves getting out in the garden too; she's great. When I clip the laurels she's really happy to do the clearing up. She doesn't mind at all.

"We grow our own garlic now and once you've tasted home grown garlic, you'll never buy the commercial stuff again, it's horrible, it smells like a damp room.

"When I get back from Tours and all the pressure and negative press that goes with them, I just go out into the garden and I think, "I don't care what people say as long as I can come home to this.

"I am a bit reclusive. I do get frightened every night I go on stage but then I always look forward to coming home; it's my holiday. I love being home for the winter with log fires and pottering around the garden. And then it'll be spring. It's all so beautiful."

www.francisrossi.com

Better Butter

Onion butter is sweet and tasty but doesn't actually contain butter, making it a great alternative for vegans; however, it's also great with meat and veggies, in pasta and even on toast and is simple to make.

It requires more time than effort - the total cooking time is roughly 24 hours.

Peel and quarter 4 lbs of onions.

Place the onions into a slow cooker with about 1/2 cup of water.

Cover the pot and heat the onions on high for several hours until they are soft, stirring occasionally.

Turn the heat down to low and continue cooking the onions until all of the liquid in them has disappeared. This can take up to 24 hours.

Cool, and then puree the onions in a food processor.

The onion butter may be frozen until ready to use.

Enjoy!

Magic of Madeira

I often use aspects of gardening and nature as analogies; like, 'whenever we sow seeds, we have faith that they will germinate but we have no idea just how fruitful they will be.' And as a result of 'sowing seeds' with the Mayor of Funchal (who is now the President of Madeira) during a reception during Chelsea Flower Show, I enjoyed a rather magical week on the Garden Island of Madeira.

Often referred to in the media as a 'Champion for Mother Nature', I am passionate about encouraging people to connect or reconnect with the many magical aspects of the natural world. Madeira was the perfect place for me to deepen and strengthen my own earthy connections and I can't recommend it highly enough for those wanting to do the same.

The people of Madeira have a long history of receiving visitors and tourists and that, together with their own reverence of nature, makes them incredibly hospitable and humble people. They are all so appreciative of their surroundings which manifests as an appreciation for life. During a relatively short stay I was lucky enough to meet local artists, restaurant and bar owners, farmers, beekeepers; go horse riding, bird watching and explore the lavadas and Laurel forests (laurissilva) as well as exchanging inspiration and ideas with the Director of Pestana Hotel Group, the Environmental Minister and, of course, the President.

There is a huge reverence for the natural elements, positive energy, creativity and sustainability all of which is embraced on the Island. They are also proud of the fact that nearly 28% of the islands energy is produced from renewable resources.

I returned home overflowing with magical memories, sights and experiences but one of the things that struck me most was how plants are allowed to 'be'. As well as the beautifully manicured public gardens, parks, and of course the famous Botanical Gardens, I witnessed nasturtiums clambering over fences, the vigorous Banana Passion Fruit entwine itself around trees, vegetables growing happily on the steepest and seemingly inaccessible slopes. Agapanthus swamp pathways and roadsides, Busy Lizzies climb up the rocky outcrops next to waterfalls and hydrangeas cling to the steep forest banks. It has inspired me to be more relaxed in my own garden and in my own life; to let things that do germinate, simply be and not to worry about the seeds that lay dormant – they too will germinate when they are ready or maybe not at all. Nature will choose.

I stayed in one of the fabulous Pestana Hotels
www.pestana.com (you can contact
pedro.tojal@pestana.com for that personal touch)
and received friendly assistance from *www.visitmadeira.pt*

You can read more about my Magical Madeiran Adventures at *www.lynneallbutt.co.uk*

Desert Gardening

I remember writing about Desert Gardening about 10 years ago, when the long-term predictions were for drought conditions. Ironically it seems that rain gardens are now far more pertinent.

A clever concept from the States, Rain Gardens are basically planted depressions or hollows that allows the absorption of rainwater runoff from impervious urban areas, like roofs, driveways, walkways, parking lots, and compacted lawn areas.

They are created with absorbent, yet free draining soil and planted with vegetation that can withstand occasional temporary flooding. Plants used are also 'light feeders', not needing many nutrients.

Green roofs, which I am also a huge advocate of, are also able to reduce rain water run-off by a whopping 60% as well as increasing natural habitat for wildlife.
Another design aspect for consideration in developed areas and which favours wildlife is the 'green seam' – simply strips of grass and shrubs that provide wildlife with a means of moving about freely and safely in urban areas.

Wouldn't it be great to see rain gardens, green roofs and green seams incorporated in newly developed areas like supermarkets, shopping malls and industrial estates?

Celebrity Chit-Chat with Beth Chatto OBE

Described as 'undoubtedly the most influential British gardener of the last half century,' Beth Chatto OBE, together with her late husband Andrew, are renowned for shaping the way we garden.

It may sound obvious now but they pioneered the concept of choosing plants for specific areas according to their natural habitat, "the right plant for the right place". This idea is brilliantly demonstrated in her earliest books titled The Dry Garden, The Damp Garden, The Gravel Garden and The Shade Garden. Beth told me, "My parents were enthusiastic gardeners but I went off to college to learn to teach. All my life I wanted to be a teacher and although it wasn't as I had intended, I suppose I have become one.

"During the War, we were looking for home for evacuees and I met Andrew. As a child he had spent a lot of time with his Uncle in California and had recognised plants like Ceanothus (Californian lilac) and Eschscholzia (Californian poppies) from his Hertfordshire home, growing wild there, rather like blackberries grow wild here.

"He wondered how they had got there from the UK and his lifelong research into plant origins, was born."

Beth continued, "When we were married, Andrew had a fruit farm and I had always wanted to have a little nursery to grow unusual plants. When he retired it rather made sense for me to take on the land.

"I don't consider myself to be a garden designer but I have been in way, as I had to design various aspects to create this garden. I have simply put the plants in the appropriate places and not just the nearest available space. I have always said that we as people wouldn't want to be thrust into the nearest job."

The Beth Chatto Gardens, in Essex, are now famous and enjoyed by a steady stream of visitors. At 88 years of age (at the time of the interview), Beth still goes out into the garden every day.

"I don't do much these days. If I sit in the chair I go to sleep which is such a bore. My staff are like extended family so we plan changes and improvements together, they think and plant like I do now. And I still meet the visitors of course."

Beth was extremely humble as she talks about the contribution her and Andrew have made to the world of horticulture.

"Three things inspired me; Andrew and the extensive research he had done about where plants came from and their preferred habitats, the flower arranging movement and a dear friend Cedric Morris whose own garden was full of treasures for me. They were species plants or wild plants and quite rare in the 1940/50's. Of course now Chelsea's full of them." she laughed, "but in those days everyone wanted big, blousy flowers. I have always liked things that are quietly vigorous and do well. The reason that some things are rare is that they're difficult.

"I must admit that I have been torn between on the one hand enjoying sharing a new range of plants through my writing but on the other hand feeling sad that the financial people have jumped on the band wagon and made it all so commercial. We must remember to take care of nature and not exploit her."

Andrew Chatto's lifelong research into plant ecology included investigating the writings of plant hunters, travellers, scientists in French and German, and he even taught himself Russian, in order to read the literature on the plant ecological associations of the USSR where many good garden plants come from.

His copious handwritten notes, poems and even hand drawn maps have recently been translated into a digital format that can be read online.

Beth explained, "When Andrew died, he never intended his writings to be published, but as time went on I thought it would be nice if someone took it on."

After discussing her thoughts with garden writer Noel Kingsbury, he put an advert in the Hardy Plant Society newsletter for volunteers who had typing skills and plant knowledge.

Out of 55 replies he selected eight people to translate and type up Andrew's notes. "I'm absolutely thrilled Andrew's work has been recognised and made available in this way. Of course it never occurred to us that it would be available online of all things."

You can find out more about the fabulous Beth Chatto Gardens and also read Andrew Chatto's papers at *www.bethchatto.co.uk.*

It was a real treat to talk to Beth, she is a remarkable woman who has achieved such great things by simply following her passion. I was thrilled when she said, "I am fascinated by the wide range of things you do; I knew you would be an interesting person to talk to. Don't leave it too long before you visit."

Kind words and high praise indeed and from a woman who has shaped horticultural history.

Wipe Out Weeds

You can create an organic weedkiller by combining four cups of vinegar to half a cup of salt and two teaspoons of washing up liquid or multiples thereof. Spray weeds with a small hand sprayer on a sunny day.

Feed Up Plants

Use the water that you have boiled pasta or veggies in to water house plants or outdoor pots as it is full of nutrients and vitamins. Leave to cool before using.

Happy Easter

Exploring why Easter's date changes every year, I learned that it is a 'moveable feast'. Easter Sunday can fall on any date from 22 March to 25 April as it is based on the lunar calendar (or cycles of the moon) rather than our more well-known solar one.

Easter always falls on the first Sunday following the full Moon (the Paschal Full Moon) after 21 March. If the Full Moon falls on a Sunday then Easter is the next Sunday.

The history of Easter reveals rich associations between the Christian faith and the practices of the early pagan religions. We are all familiar with the traditional symbols of bunnies, chicks and off course Easter eggs but I particularly like the faery-lore that suggests to leave food and drink out for the fairies on the nights of our festivals; it is believed that if the fairies are not honoured with gifts at these times, they will work mischief in our lives.

Fairy's have favourite foods for each festival and for Ostara, or Easter, it is customary to leave something sweet like honey, mead or candy. Perhaps a gift of sweets corresponds to the sweet nectar gathered from new spring flowers, who knows but it does seem a good trade to stay a mischief-free zone.

New spring growth, and the promises it holds, also reflects our own blossoming and the benefits of new beginnings at this time of year as we shed off the old winter energy and feel the sap rise.

It is a good time to 'spring into action' and re-evaluate jobs, relationships, living situations and all lifestyle choices.

It seems to me that Spring is not only a season; it is a state of mind.

Choc shocks ... did you know?

- Easter eggs for 2014 went on sale in some supermarkets on Christmas Eve 2013.

- The 2012 survey Easter Egg Packaging by Jo Swinson MP found that only 38% of the average Easter egg box is actually Easter egg. The rest is paper and plastic. Commercial Easter eggs are responsible for up to 3,000 tonnes of waste. Nestlé however announced in 2012 that they have become the first major confectioner to achieve 100% recyclability in its entire Easter egg packaging range across the UK and Ireland.

- Dieticians are warning that eating five Easter eggs (the average given to most children) plus the bars of chocolate included with them, could see youngsters doubling their recommended calorie intake for a week and seeing their weight increase by several pounds within days. The recommended daily amounts are around 2,000 calories a day for an average 11-year-old boy and 1,500 for a girl, but many could be eating up to 10,000 calories over the Easter period.

Ley Line Lore

There are many different explanations for ley lines; they are also known as 'Fairy Paths', (Irish) 'Dragon Paths', (Chinese) and 'Song Lines', (Australian Aborigine) and every tradition and culture throughout the world has their own explanations of them. Even though the term 'Ley-line' was originally conceived by Alfred 'Watkins, by 1929, he discarded the use of the name 'ley' and referred to his alignments only as 'old straight tracks' or 'archaic tracks'.

These tracks, or geometrical lines that run across landscapes are extremely powerful energy zones, often creating vortexes of energy (dimensional spiraling energies) where they meet or cross -like the meridians and chakra points in our own body and energy field. Ley lines can also have a negative side. It is thought that when the energy from a ley line passes through decaying matter such as a city dump, a polluted river or a graveyard it picks up the negative influences it encounters. The energy becomes what geomancers call a 'black stream'.

Similarly, geological fissures and fault lines can also interfere with the earth energy and are often referred to as black streams of energy or geopathic stress lines.

The term geopathic stress literally means 'illness produced from the earth'. These black streams or negative energy lines do not directly cause illness however they can affect the way we function particularly if we spend a lot of time in a geopathic stress area such as a working environment, our home and in particular where we sleep. During our sleep cells need to be renewed, nutrients absorbed, and food digested but if you are laying over a geopathic stress line your body will use its energy to ward off the effects of geopathic stress weakening your immune system and allowing disease (dis-ease) to take hold.

Electromagnetic fields (EMF) are man-made and mainly caused by power-induced electrical appliances and installations, including TV's, VDU's, microwave ovens and mobile phones and also create their own form of electromagnetic stress.

Electromagnetic stress can have the same effect on the brains vibrations as geopathic stress, leading to health problems and a lowered immune system. In addition to external influences, we live with and can contribute to negative energies; it is part of our daily life.

A bad thought, action or comment can set up an area of negativity that will start to feed off any further conflict around it until it becomes large enough to start influencing people's moods. You will no doubt have experienced an area or house just has an unhappy or angry atmosphere. So how can you find out if geopathic stress is affecting you and what can you do about it?

Intuition is the key. Intuition is literally 'tuition from within' and we all have the ability to 'intuit' but tend not to use it.

Have a think - are there areas you feel uncomfortable in? Where does the cat sleep? Or the dog?

Cats like areas of geopathic stress whereas dogs will avoid it.

Outdoors, Nature is a great indicator. Gnarled trees or branches that are unnaturally twisted and contorted, plants that don't grow well or even die for no obvious reason can be indicators of geopathic stress. There may be problems with mould in the house or a lot of lichen or moss growing on the roof, walls, or lawn as geopathic stress encourages the growth of these.

There may also be problems with ants, wasps or bees. Whilst most animals avoid GS, some, like bees, wasps, ants and cats are attracted to it. Large ant nests are often on crossings of underground streams, while ant paths often follow streams too.

Bare patches in lawns, moss and fungi, stunted or mutated growth in veggie gardens particularly lie (or fall) on edge lines of geopathic stress. Ivy, bindweed, nettles, dock thistles, foxgloves, ferns and nightshades are attracted to, and thrive in, geopathic stress and gaps in hedges may indicate the position of a line of geopathic stress crossing the hedge. The presence of springs and wells can also increase the likelihood of geopathic stress.

Other indicators can include feeling better when away from home. For instance, a condition may clear up or improve when away on holiday only to come back again when you get back home. Waking up feeling unrefreshed or feeling worse in the mornings can be due to being affected by geopathic stress in bed as the body's resistance to it drops to a third of normal during sleep.

Often babies who are restless in their sleep will be trying to avoid geopathic stress. When babies were monitored, they all slept peacefully after their cots were moved to a geopathic stress free place.

Austrian Kathe Bachler has also researched the effects of geopathic stress in a classroom to find it can be responsible for many behavioural and learning problems experienced by children. When their desk is affected by a stress zone it may affect the concentration and mood of the school child. Bachler found that 95% of failed examinations were due to the presence of zones of disturbance. She suggests a 'rotating classroom' be adopted, where seating positions are changed regularly, and found it resulted in better attention spans and interest in learning, improved thinking and memory and ultimately improved school performance generally.

Ironically, I think one of the reasons that little consideration is given to the possible presence of geopathic stress is that many of the symptoms can easily be attributed to a more familiar type of stress-like work, an unhappy family life or just 'typical teenage mood swings' but of course it could be the geopathic stress that is causing or contributing to those states in the first place.

There are several ways it can be addressed, involving dowsing, bespoke products or by simply moving your bed. To find out more, by all means email me or have a look at the information available on the internet. It is a fascinating subject that probably affects most of us and is worth investigating.

After reading that bees prefer areas of geopathic stress, I have always dowsed to find a suitable site for hives and also when collecting swarms.

All the swarms I have collected have been in an area where at least two ley lines cross but often more. I have read that bait hives placed on crossing ley lines will also be more successful in attracting swarms though haven't tried it yet.

As credible as I find it, I also continue to be amazed by the consistency of the results and I know there are numerous bee keepers who adopt the same practise. After keeping bees for a number of years, I now consider myself to be a 'natural and extensive beekeeper' - one who keeps bees for pleasure. A beekeeper who keeps bees for product or profit is known as an 'intensive beekeeper'.

And I even prefer to pop to a more 'intensive' beekeeper for my honey rather than to take the honey from my own little apiary.

Photograph by Adele Nozedar.

The author barefoot beekeeping.

A single honey bee worker produces just ¹⁄₁₂ of a teaspoon of honey in her lifetime.

Berry Interesting

Did you know that peanuts are beans; and from a botanical point of view, avocados and pumpkins are fruits, not vegetables, because they bear the plants' seeds.

Rhubarb, on the other hand, is a vegetable and a pineapple is a berry.

Wake Up and Smell the Coffee

Old coffee grinds make great plant food. Simply place a handful of coffee grinds (or grounds) into a bucket of water, leave for a day or two to create a nice amber-coloured liquid and use to feed plants accordingly.

There are numerous other uses for the coffee waste too.

- Sprinkle on flower beds to deter slugs, ants and even cats.
- Use on a damp cloth to scour away grease and grime.
- The addition of coffee grounds to hydrangeas is good for blue blooms. Blueberries, cranberries, and citrus fruits also like coffee added to their soil and other coffee-loving plants include camellias, gardenias, rhododendrons.
- They can even be used as a gentle exfoliant for your body and face.

Wonderful Wordle

If you love words you will adore Wordle, a toy for generating "word clouds" from text that you provide. The clouds give greater prominence to words that appear more frequently in the source text that you use.

You can provide words or far more revealing is to let Wordle create a cloud from the words you most often use on your computer. (See mine below as an example).

Have a go at www.wordle.net

Law and (no) Order

There are some weird laws out there ...

- In New Jersey, cabbage can't be sold on Sunday.
- In California, it is illegal to set a mouse trap without a hunting license.
- In Texas, it is illegal to milk another person's cow.
- In Oklahoma, people who make "ugly faces" at dogs may be fined and/or jailed.
- In London, it is illegal to flag down a taxi if you have the plague.
- It is a legal requirement in Milan to smile at all times, with funerals and hospital visits being the exception.
- In Alaska, waking a sleeping bear for a photo opportunity is strictly forbidden.
- And finally, a reminder not to believe all you read; I read that in Iceland it is forbidden to run a Marathon in less than 3 hours 30 minutes. I know this not to be true as in 2005 I ran the Reykjavik marathon in just over 4 hours. Although to be honest, anything over 4 hours is affectionately referred to as 'tourist time' by the seasoned runners.

The best advice for marathon running was given to me by fellow bee-keeper and TV presenter, Bill Turnbull who said: "Start off slow ... and get slower."

Nappy-ness

Placing a clean nappy in the bottom of a hanging basket, before adding compost, will help retain moisture during the season.

Healthy Leather

For a healthy, tasty treat, try fruit leather. Despite the dubious sounding name, it's not something used to make a hedgerow harness or a strawberry saddle, but a highly nutritious, energising and easy to make snack.

Simmer 1kg chopped crab apples and 1kg mixed hedgerow berries (other fruit can be used depending what's in season or preferred) with a little water until everything is soft. Drain off the juice and push the rest through a sieve. Add 2 tablespoons sugar to the pulp and simmer to reduce down by 20%. Spread thinly (about 2ml) on a lined baking tray. Put in the oven on a very low temperature until you can peel the fruit cleanly away from the backing.

You can add fillings like softened cream cheese, cheese spreads, jam, preserves, marmalade, or peanut butter for variety.

Oil be Blowed

Did you know crisps make fabulous fire lighters? Some varieties will ignite and burn quicker than others (the ones that you 'pop and can't stop' are the best). So next time you go camping don't forget the crisps!

Working with Elementals

Fancy making gardening a bit easier? Then enlist the help of the elementals and devas. I have been working with them for a number of years. I have also worked with a couple of Divas but that is an entirely different thing!

The word deva comes from the Sanskrit language, meaning "a being of brilliant light" and is used to indicate a nonphysical being. Personally I use 'deva' as a general name for nature spirits.

Devas have an instinctive knowledge; they do not have to acquire knowledge like we do. They have instinctive knowledge of cosmic patterns, relationships, and harmonies and as such are great to collaborate with, making fabulous work colleagues.

Whilst everything in existence has its own spiritual aspect, some are quite inert and others can be very active. For example the spiritual presence of a storm or a piece of music can be felt by everyone, yet the spirit of a computer or tarmac road is not so obviously tangible but present nonetheless and shouldn't be overlooked.

To collaborate with the devas, simply ask for their help in certain tasks. They are not restricted to the garden or even outdoors – there are devas who can help with technical stuff, travel and even housework. I have noticed that when the devas are invited to be involved, the task in hand goes much more smoothly and even quicker.

I have also 'negotiated' with the devas with a regard to a lawnmower that refused to start by explaining if it didn't want to do the job then I would have to replace it with one that did. After our 'chat', the mower started on the second pull much to the amazement of several sceptical onlookers.

Obviously there are many people who are sceptical about Nature Spirits but the good news is that the elementals are not so judgemental about us; so I would invite you just to try communicating and see what happens.

As Elbert Hubbard said, "The supernatural is the natural not yet understood."

Nature Knows Best

And Finally ...

Both of my Granddads (and even great Granddads) were professional gardeners and although I only ever knew one Nan (Moosh), she was incredibly nature-wise and influential, nurturing essential attributes like common sense as well as sharing much of her knowledge, for which I will always be grateful.

Also much gratitude to Mum (Carol) who has passed on her love of gardening and nature as well as many recipes and advice like, "If it sets, use it as jam, if it doesn't, use it as a cordial."

And of course to my brother Ian, who as I have said before, 'keeps my feet firmly on the ground as only a brother can'. We still work together occasionally and I look forward to those days of humour (and hard work) very much.

Much gratitude also goes to artist and creative, Karin Mear for her beautiful line drawings, which add life to the Allsortium, for the cover and for interpreting my requests so intuitively. You can find Karin on Facebook.

Special thanks to Steve Thomas, for not only undertaking the immense technical aspects of getting this particular dream into print but more so for the continuous support and encouragement. And adding much enjoyment along the way.

I feel it appropriate to mention my appreciation for all the animals and pets I have learned from and how important and instrumental their companionship has been during various stages of my life, especially Tippy my canine companion for over 14 years and whom I was heartbroken to lose five years ago. Yogi the Westie now continues the valuable teachings along with my 2 pigs, 8 chickens, drake, my bees and Mother Nature herself.

And of course, I will always be deeply indebted to my father, Bob, also a professional and gifted gardener and who encouraged me to start my own gardening business at 17 years old. He also taught me to prune roses when I was 6 and instilled a strong work ethic in both myself and my brother, suggesting that if we had nothing to do then we dug a hole in the ground and filled it back in. It has done neither of us any harm. Sadly, Dad passed away in 1996 and has gone on to develop even greater landscapes, but his passion for the outdoors is impeccably immortalised.

Lynne Allbutt.

All Lynne Allbutt publications are available from Amazon or *www.lynneallbutt.com.*

The author is also available for informative and inspirational talks. See *www.lynneallbutt.com* for details.

Other books by Lynne Allbutt include:

Barefoot and Before.

At the age of 47, Lynne Allbutt decided to see if she could run across a country, barefoot.

Far from being an ultra runner or extreme sports enthusiast, Lynne is a gardener and beekeeper. However, she is also a creator and pursuer of personal challenges.

'Barefoot and Before' chronicles her running journey and also revisits personal aspects of her life with honest recollections and appraisals of the highs and lows of both. Follow her inspiring journey through an ever- changing landscape as she confronts her deepest fears and embraces vulnerability.

"Running the mountainous width of Wales is an impressive undertaking in shoes, let alone without. Well done."
- Sir Ranulph Fiennes.

If U ....?

… could ask anyone just one question, who and what would you ask?

A little book of light-hearted and enlightening questions to stimulate and surprise in a pull-out, pocket-sized format.

Personali-trees.

Discover what your favourite tree, flower or shrub reveals about you.

Made in the USA
Charleston, SC
27 November 2015